JASLEEN KAUR

Letters to my Twins

A Mother's Journey of Becoming

Dedication

To my beloved children. I consider myself the most fortunate mother to raise such extraordinary little souls. May this book remind you that you are loved unconditionally.

To the new generation—there is no love like that of siblings. Though separated by visa constraints and ocean distances, may you cultivate bonds that nurture love through generations to come.

To new moms—I see you. I understand how hard it is. Your struggles are valid. You are not alone.

How We Survive

Last night you cried for me at 3 a.m.
*   and I couldn't remember my own name.*

Just "Mama"—
*   endless,*
*   exhausted,*
*   everything.*

They say motherhood is a blessing, and it is—
*   but they don't tell you about the breaking,*
*   the impossible mathematics of*
*   two babies, two hands,*
*   one mother disappearing into their needs.*

Some days I mourn the woman I was,
*   the one who finished thoughts mid-sentence,*
*   who showered without an audience,*
*   who believed she knew what tired meant.*

Your Papa held me when I whispered
*   "I can't do this anymore"—*
*   words I was terrified to speak aloud,*
*   ashamed that love could coexist with drowning.*
*   He is my anchor,*

my breath between the waves,
the reason I can stand and become.

And there were others—
grandparents who cooked so we wouldn't go hungry,
friends who left food on the doorstep when pneumonia took us all,
mothers in a WhatsApp group who let me fall apart without judgment,
a stranger in the grocery store whose eyes met mine—
my hands impossibly full, my composure crumbling—
and without a word, she gave me the look that said:
"I see you. It's going to be okay."

Not everyone understood.
Not everyone saw.
But those who did—
those small mercies—
they were everything.

This is how we survive:
We lose ourselves completely.
We find ourselves in their eyes.
We break. We shatter. We become.
We love in ways that terrify us,
in ways that remake us entirely.

For every parent who has ever felt lost and found in the same breath,
who loves fiercely while falling apart,
who whispers in the dark: you are not alone.
Your exhaustion is valid.

Your love is enough.
You are enough—
even when you're breaking,
especially when you're becoming.

PREFACE

Dear Reader,

In your hands, you hold not just a book, but a tapestry of devotion, woven with words, memories, and dreams. This collection of letters began only as a whisper of an idea when two tiny heartbeats flickered on an ultrasound screen, transforming my husband's (Danvir) and my world in an instant. Those pulsing dots on the monitor were our babies - referred to clinically as "Baby A" and "Baby B." But to us, they were already so much more.

In that moment of wonder and anticipation, we chose to call them "Momo" and "Panipuri" for the duration of my pregnancy - names inspired by my favorite foods, infusing warmth and cultural significance into the sterile medical terms. These endearing nicknames would later evolve into Tara and Dhruv, but the love and excitement they represent remained constant throughout our journey.

This book chronicles that journey through handwritten letters, starting from the early days of pregnancy in Newton, Massachusetts. I vividly remember the day we announced our pregnancy to our family on May 9, 2021, and the mixture of surprise and delight on their faces when we clarified that we weren't adopting another cat, but expecting a human baby. The thought still brings a smile to my face.

Danvir and my path took an unexpected turn when, at just 11

weeks pregnant, we made the monumental decision to move from Boston to California for his new job. This move, while exciting, meant leaving behind a treasured network of friends who had become our family away from home. I think of Darsana, Anaya, Sid, Sanya, Raj, Siya, Vishal, Kiara, Nakul, Kriti, Bhavik, Kush, and Abi - friends who threw us a surprise farewell party that left us in tears of gratitude. Their love and support during those early, uncertain days of pregnancy were invaluable, and their presence is felt throughout these letters.

As we embarked on our new life in California, we began building new connections. I recall meeting Sameer and Mira, Shriya and Ravi, and the joy of introducing our unborn babies to the 6-week-old daughter of Vinay and Namita, our twin's future best friend, Ria. These new friendships, formed as our family was just beginning, have become an integral part of our story.

But even with all of that being said, this book is more than just a collection of letters written to our twins, capturing moments big and small, from pregnancy cravings and baby showers to first steps and toddler tantrums. It's a reflection on the transformative power of parenthood, the challenges of balancing personal ambitions with family life, and the beautiful complexity of cultural identity in a globalized world. As an Indian woman pursuing a PhD in Public Policy in the United States, my path to motherhood was intertwined with academic pursuits, cultural adjustments, and the forging of new relationships far from home. These letters document both my children's growth and also my own evolution - as a mother, a scholar, a wife, and an individual striving to bridge multiple worlds.

Throughout these pages, you'll find stories of triumph and struggle, of sleepless nights and celebrated milestones. You'll meet a cast of characters – grandparents, aunts, uncles, and friends – who form the global village that has supported and celebrated our family across continents. You'll see reflections on the bittersweet nature of immigration, the strength found in maintaining cultural roots, and the excitement of creating new traditions. These letters speak to the hopes and fears all parents harbor for their children, the delicate balance of preserving one's identity while embracing change, and the profound ways in which love reshapes our world.

Our family's story, unique as it is, resonates with universal themes that will strike a chord with a diverse array of readers. Parents of twins will find solidarity in the double challenges and rewards of raising two little ones simultaneously, and all parents, regardless of their children's ages, will recognize the deep affection, the sleepless nights, the overwhelming responsibility, and the indescribable fulfillment that comes with raising a child. And readers from any generation will connect with the timeless themes of love, family, personal growth, and the search for identity and belonging.

This is not just a book for new parents or those expecting; it's for anyone who has ever loved deeply, faced life's uncertainties with courage, or strived to build a bridge between cultures. It's also for the dreamers and the doers, the ones who've left home to chase ambitions, and those who've found home in unexpected places. In sharing our story, I hope to illuminate the common threads that bind us all in the tapestry of human experience.

To Tara and Dhruv, my dear Momo and Panipuri, these letters are a testament to the love that surrounded you from the very beginning. To my fellow parents, may you find echoes of your own journey in these pages. And to all readers, I hope this book offers a window into the beautiful, chaotic, and deeply rewarding adventure of parenthood in a multicultural world.

As you turn these pages, I invite you to join our family's journey – to laugh with us, to ponder life's big questions, and to celebrate the small moments that make life extraordinary. For in the end, it is these moments, strung together with love and intention, that create the masterpiece of a family's story.

With warmth and gratitude,

Jasleen

Cultural & Family Reference Guide

This book includes Indian family terms and cultural references that are woven throughout our daily lives. I've provided this guide so you can better understand the relationships and traditions that shape our world.

Maternal Side (Jasleen's Family)

- Nani – Maternal grandmother (Jasleen's mother, Inderjeet Kaur)
- Nanu – Maternal grandfather (Jasleen's father)
- Mamu – Maternal uncle (Jasleen's brother)
- Masi – Maternal aunt (Jasleen's sister or close friend considered family)
- Choti Nani – Jasleen's maternal and paternal aunt (literally "small grandmother"), younger than the maternal grandmother
- Badi Nani – Jasleen's maternal and paternal aunt (literally "big grandmother"), older than the maternal grandmother
- Mataji – Great-grandmother (Jasleen's grandmother)

Paternal Side (Danvir's Family)

- Dadi – Paternal grandmother (Danvir's mother, Virinder Kaur)

- Dadu – Paternal grandfather (Danvir's father)
- Chachu – Paternal uncle (Danvir's younger brother)
- Chachi – Paternal aunt by marriage
- Tayaji – Paternal uncle (Danvir's older brother, Hardik)
- Tayiji – Paternal aunt by marriage (Hardik's wife, Purba)
- Choti Dadi – Danvir's maternal and paternal aunt (literally "small grandmother"), younger than the paternal grandmother
- Badi Dadi – Danvir's maternal and paternal aunt (literally "big grandmother"), older than the paternal grandmother

Immediate Family

- Papa/Dad – Father (Danvir Singh Sethi)
- Mama/Mom/Amma – Mother (Jasleen Kaur)

Cultural & Religious Terms

- Gurdwara – Sikh temple
- Kirtan/Shabad Kirtan – Devotional Sikh hymns
- Langar – Community kitchen/meal served at Gurdwara

Indian Festival & Celebration Terms

- Lohri – North Indian harvest festival celebrated in January
- Gurupurab – Sikh holy day celebrating a Guru's birthday

Note: In Indian culture, it's common to use relationship titles as names (like calling your grandmother "Nani" instead of her first name). Many close family friends are also given familial titles as a sign of respect and affection, which is why some "uncles" and "aunts" mentioned are not blood relatives.

<h1 style="text-align:center">August 28, 2021</h1>

Dear Tara and Dhruv,

Tomorrow morning, your Papa and I will learn your biological sex, and the excitement in our family is palpable. We've even created a Google form for family and friends to predict whether you'll be girls, boys, or one of each. Your Masi, my dear friend who's like an aunt to you, wisely pointed out that while we commonly use the term "gender reveal," gender is actually a social construct. Perhaps by the time you're adults, we'll have found a more appropriate term – maybe "sex reveal"?

This anticipation has led me to reflect deeply on the complexities of gender in our society. My studies in gender and my personal experiences as a woman in both Indian and American contexts have made me acutely aware of the challenges faced by both women and men in our world.

I've pondered the obstacles that girls and women often face – the subtle and not-so-subtle discrimination that can permeate various aspects of life, from education and career opportunities to social expectations and personal safety. There were moments when I worried about these challenges when I thought about the possibility of both of you being girls.

But I've also recognized the unique difficulties boys and men encounter in our society. The pressure to conform to traditional masculinity, the expectation to be emotionally stoic, and the challenges in expressing vulnerability are burdens that weigh heavily on many men. Your Papa's perspective has been instrumental in broadening my understanding of these issues. He's shared his own experiences of feeling pressured to always be strong, to hide his emotions, and to conform to society's narrow definition of masculinity. His openness has helped me see that gender expectations can be equally constraining for men, albeit in different ways.

As I've grappled with these thoughts, I've realized that the patriarchal setup impacts everyone, regardless of gender. This realization has been both enlightening and somewhat over-whelming. How do we, as parents, prepare you for a world that can be both beautiful and challenging?

I'll admit, there have been moments when I've had fleeting preferences for your genders. The idea of shopping for sparkly girls' clothes or imagining spa days with a daughter has its appeal. And in a household with your Papa and our cat Oreo, the thought of having a girl to balance the energy is enticing.

But here's the beautiful truth I've come to embrace: regard-less of your sex or gender, your Papa and I will be thrilled. Whether you're girls, boys, or one of each, we'll love you fiercely and unconditionally. We'll encourage you to explore all your interests, whether that's shopping trips or sports, art or science, regardless of societal gender norms.

What matters most is that you're healthy, happy, and know you're deeply loved. We're excited about all the adventures we'll share – bedtime stories, family outings, and watching you discover the world. These experiences aren't defined by gender, but by the delight of being together.

Your Papa, whom I adore for his wonderful neutrality in this matter, reads stories to you every night. Well, to be precise, he reads to my belly where you are nestled! We've been borrowing loads of children's books from the library, and your Papa's animated storytelling never fails to make me smile. We've even recorded some of these sessions for you to watch when you're older. I can't wait for you to see how thrilled we were to meet you, even before you were born!

As for me, I find myself praying for your well-being each day. Our friends and family, who affectionately call us "JasDan," are already so eager to meet you. Nani, Mataji, and Dadi – are even knitting the most adorable unisex sweaters!

As we await your arrival, our hearts overflow with affection. We're honored and humbled that you chose us as your parents. Our lives have been enriched beyond measure by your impending arrival.

Love always,

Mama

P.S. Years from now, when you read this, I hope you remember that parenthood is a journey of constant growth. Our understanding evolves, our perspectives expand, and our love deepens with each passing day. When I go back and read some of these letters, I sometimes feel amazed, sometimes embarrassed, and sometimes tempted to delete a few things. But I choose not to. I want to remain true to every version of myself — the confident and the unsure, the graceful and the flawed. Each version reflects a moment in time, and each one has helped me grow. I want to honor that evolution rather than erase it. If, when you are older, you read something that doesn't align with your values, or with the society and culture you live in, I promise I will listen. I will want to understand your perspective. After all, life is about change — about learning, unlearning, and growing. Through all that change, though, one thing will remain constant: my love for you and your Papa. And my commitment to having a heart and mind open enough to evolve, to learn, to accept, to acknowledge — and to stand by you, no matter what.

P.P.S. I have a little secret to share. When I filled out our family prediction form, I voted for girl/girl. Not because I preferred that outcome, but because I noticed all the votes were split between boy/boy and boy/girl. I wanted to ensure that if we had twin girls, they would see that someone had predicted and celebrated their arrival, too. It's a small thing, but it reflects my hope that you'll always feel equally valued and loved, no matter who you grow up to be.

January 11, 2022

Dearest Tara and Dhruv,

Now that we've settled into some semblance of a routine at home, I finally feel ready to write down the incredible story of how you came into this world. It's taken me over a month to find both the mental clarity and emotional space to capture this journey - the whirlwind of your birth, our five days in the hospital, and these first weeks at home have been unlike anything I could have imagined.

On a Sunday in early December, I was admitted to the hospital due to a condition called preeclampsia, which causes high blood pressure during pregnancy. You were 34 weeks and 6 days along at that point. The maternal fetal medicine specialists informed us that your arrival was imminent. However, my heart wasn't ready; I wanted you to grow stronger inside me for a bit longer. They kept me connected to a fetal monitoring machine called a Non-Stress Test (NST). The doctors recommended injecting me with steroids to help your lungs develop more quickly, in the event of premature birth. Being your mother, I was determined to make the best decision for you. I delved into academic research papers, meticulously analyzing the information while lying in my hospital bed, before finally agreeing to the treatment.

The NST results were promising, and my blood pressure stabilized. The doctors allowed me to go home two days later to celebrate my birthday, under the condition that I would return daily for NST and laboratory tests. These tests were crucial to monitor my liver function, as preeclampsia and another condition called cholestasis were affecting my overall health and well-being.

Three days later, which coincided with Gurupurab, an important Sikh holiday, your Dadi prepared delicious aloo parathas (potato-stuffed flatbreads) for breakfast. After enjoying this meal, Dadi and I headed to the Mountain View clinic for my tests. We avoided the main hospital due to a nurses' strike that day. During the check-up, my blood pressure soared to 172 - an alarmingly high number!

After 30 minutes of monitoring, Dr. Brown, my gynecologist, delivered unexpected news: "You are delivering your babies today. Your blood pressure is very high. Ask your spouse to get your hospital bag and take you directly to the Santa Clara hospital. I've informed them, and they're ready for you. You can't eat or drink anything from now on. Tell your husband to hurry, and no *dilly-dallying*." Even in that tense moment, the word "dilly-dallying" brought a smile to my face!

I immediately called your Papa, while Dadi contacted your Tayaji, Hardik. Looking back, I wish someone had informed my parents right away, but in the rush of events, I'm not sure when or how they were told. Everything unfolded so rapidly!

Your Papa arrived as quickly as he could, meeting us in the parking lot and arranging for a cab to take Dadi home. Before leaving, she reassured us with a comforting phrase in Punjabi: "Babaji sab theek karange" (God will take care of everything).

In the hospital parking lot, your Papa and I paused for a

moment. We held hands, exchanged a quiet kiss, and took a couple of minutes to acknowledge the new journey we were about to begin before heading toward the labor and delivery unit.

But before we went in, I did something that still makes me pause when I think about it: I shaved my face.

I had quite a bit of facial hair, and I didn't want the newborn hospital pictures to capture me that way.

No one asked me to shave. The nurses didn't mention it. Your Papa didn't suggest it. Dr. Brown certainly didn't include it in her instructions to rush to the hospital. And yet there I was — in a medical emergency, my blood pressure dangerously high, about to deliver you both prematurely — thinking about facial hair.

At the time, I told myself it was about "gathering myself" or "feeling in control." And maybe part of it was. But looking back, I wonder how much of it was truly about control — and how much was about the way I had been conditioned to believe the world expects women to look. Neat. Groomed. Presentable. Even when being rushed into emergency surgery. Even when our bodies are in crisis. Even in the most vulnerable, raw moments of our lives.

It seems like such a small detail, and yet it reveals something profound about the invisible expectations women carry. We are taught to monitor our appearance constantly, to stay aware of how we are being seen, to manage how we look for the comfort or approval of others. These messages run so deep that they operate automatically — even in moments when they should be completely irrelevant.

Was I doing it for myself? Or because I had internalized the belief that women must look a certain way — that we must be picture-ready even in our most medical, surgical, vulnerable moments? How much of what I called "gathering myself" was actually quiet compliance with expectations I didn't even realize I was following?

I think about that moment often now. Not with regret, exactly — but with a kind of sad awareness. In one of the most significant moments of my life — about to meet you both, about to become your mother — part of my mental space was occupied by thoughts about facial hair and photographs and how I would appear to the world. That is what we often do to women. We teach them that appearance matters as much as — sometimes more than — their actual lived experience.

[When you were about three months old, a close family member once told me that "my facial hair would hurt your skin when I hugged and kissed you." I remember freezing in that moment, unable to respond. I have replayed that conversation in my head many times since, thinking of what I wish I had said. I could have said, "Danvir has facial hair too — but you've never told him it might hurt the babies. Why is it easier to comment on mine simply because I am a woman?" Or, "That is a painful thing to say to a new mother who is already carrying insecurities and doing her very best. Why make her feel guilty for hugging her own children?"

Growing up, there was constant commentary about how I looked — my facial hair, the shape of my teeth, my weight when I gained it, my weight when I lost it. In India, people often speak freely about a woman's body, rarely pausing to consider how it might make her feel. One thing I have deeply appreciated about living in the United States is the relative freedom from that constant scrutiny. Yes, people here can be individualistic — but I choose that, every day, over living in a space where others feel entitled to evaluate my body, my clothes, or whether my purpose should be to "lose the baby weight" after raising twins.

My confidence had suffered for years. It slowly returned here — especially after becoming your Papa's wife. He loves me in every version: on days I feel insecure, on days I feel strong; with full body hair, with weight gain, with weight loss. With him, I can admit my insecurities — and somehow that safety has made me more secure. Still, that comment shook me. Eventually, after I finished breastfeeding you, I chose to get laser hair removal and to straighten my teeth with retainers — choices that were mine, but shaped by a lifetime of messages about how I should look.][1]

I'm sharing this not to burden you, but to help you recognize these forces when they operate in your own lives. I want you to be able to ask yourselves: Am I doing this for me? Or because I've been taught this is what's expected? Is this self-care — or is it performance for an audience I never invited?

After that brief pause, we finally headed into the labor and delivery unit.

As Dr. Brown had said, the hospital staff was expecting us. But the nurses seemed new, perhaps not fully trained, and their flustered energy made me feel overwhelmed — or maybe it was the magnesium they were giving me to control my blood pressure. Even now, I'm not entirely sure

In a tender moment, your Papa suggested, "I think we should name Panipuri now." We had already settled on Tara for Momo - girl names had come so easily to us - But boy names? They

---

[1] The paragraphs in parentheses were written later, during the editing and formatting of this book, and were not part of the original letter written that day.

had proven surprisingly elusive, and we'd spent months deliberating without finding the perfect fit. Without hesitation, I responded from the depths of my heart, "Dhruv, my DhruvTara, my stars who will shine bright and light up our lives".

When your Papa went to move the car from temporary parking to the permanent garage, I felt a wave of fear wash over me. The magnesium was causing intense heat in my body, and being alone amplified my anxiety. The prospect of a c-section and being cut open terrified me. I was also worried that it might be too soon for you to be born.

In that vulnerable moment, a Punjabi nurse approached me. She held my hands and offered words of comfort: "Your babies are going to be born on the auspicious day of Gurupurab. You and your babies are special, and the world is celebrating them." She explained to another nurse, "Just like Christmas is for you, Gurupurab is for us." Her words brought me a sense of peace and connection to my culture, even in this foreign hospital setting.

They moved me to the operating theater before your Papa returned. I insisted on waiting for him, and they assured me it would take some time to prepare me for surgery. The room was spacious and blindingly bright. Just as we were about to begin, the surgeon received an urgent call - a pipe had burst in his house, and he had to leave immediately!

By the time this setback was resolved, your Papa had returned, all geared up in surgical attire. Our new doctor was Dr. Nora, who was incredibly kind. She held my hands, assuring me that I was in good hands and that they would take excellent care of me and you both. She patiently explained the procedure and helped position me for the spinal block.

Your Papa stood beside me, and together we prepared to welcome you into the world. The anesthesiologist, whose name

I regrettably don't remember, was exceptional. Not only did he administer the spinal block skillfully, but he also helped calm my nerves. He even took on the role of photographer, capturing those first precious moments in the operating room.

Everything happened so quickly after that. Tara, you were born at 3:36 pm PST. When they whisked you away to check your vitals, I panicked, asking, "Why isn't she crying?" The anesthesiologist reassured me, "It's not exactly like in the movies, you know! Give her time, she will cry." And oh, did you cry! Your strong voice filled the room moments later.

Dhruv, you followed at 3:39 pm PST. This time, knowing not to expect immediate Hollywood-style crying, I simply smiled, filled with love and anticipation.

Your Papa went to you both, cutting your umbilical cords – your final physical connection to me. The nurses cleaned and swaddled you, then handed you to Papa. When he brought you to me, I was overcome with emotion. Tears streamed down my face as I beheld your tiny, perfect forms. Dhruv, you weighed 4 pounds and 10 ounces, while Tara, you were exactly 4 pounds. Papa managed to cradle you both in one arm as the anesthesiologist captured a photo of the four of us – our new family, embarking on a journey filled with triumphs, sorrows, adventures, and boundless love.

After the surgery, they moved us to the recovery room, where we would stay for the next five days. They checked my temperature, which had dropped dangerously low to 34.4°C (94°F). They quickly covered me with blankets and heat pads, and placed you both in warmers. It was a tense few hours until all our temperatures normalized, and everyone in the room breathed a collective sigh of relief.

Our Five Days in the Hospital:

What followed were five days that felt both eternal and fleeting. The magnesium they continued giving me for my preeclampsia left me feeling like I was moving through thick fog. I was groggy, nauseous, and tethered to a catheter - hardly the glowing new mother I'd imagined myself to be. The euphoria of your arrival battled constantly with the physical misery of my own recovery.

Learning to breastfeed felt like an impossible puzzle. You both cried so much, and I felt utterly helpless. Here I was, supposed to have some maternal instinct kick in, but instead I felt clumsy and defeated. Your Papa, exhausted as he was, would wake up every time you stirred and take care of you both. The nurses kept praising him: "He swaddles better than most moms!" they'd exclaim with amazement.

The irony wasn't lost on me - here was a society that expects mothers to intuitively know everything about baby care, yet the nurses seemed shocked that a father could master something as basic as swaddling. But their praise of your Papa, while well-intentioned, began a pattern that would follow us home. Everyone - nurses, doctors, visitors, even our own parents - couldn't stop marveling at what an "amazing husband" I had. And yes, he was amazing. He was devoted, attentive, and tireless. But somehow, in all the celebration of his contributions, my own seemed to disappear.

Another American hospital quirk that baffled me: I was given three meals a day, snacks, and even ice cream, all included in our stay. But your Papa? He had to fend for himself or go hungry. This strange system seemed to acknowledge that the birthing parent needed nourishment to recover, but completely ignored that the other parent was just as sleep-deprived, just as emotionally invested, and just as much in need of support.

We returned home five days later. Your homecoming was beautiful - the house was decorated with balloons and glitter garlands, thanks to your Dadu's efforts. When we arrived, Dadu came down to help. Papa and Dadu carried you in your car seats up the stairs, as I could barely walk. Dadi opened the door to welcome us, pouring mustard oil on both sides of the entrance - a tradition considered auspicious in our culture.

The love that surrounded us in that moment was overwhelming. My heart overflowed with emotion, even as exhaustion weighed heavily on your Papa and me. For the next 25 days, Dadi and Dadu took charge of nearly everything. I focused solely on caring for you, pumping milk, feeding you, and singing to you. I didn't even change a diaper or learn how to buckle a car seat during that time!

My recovery was incredibly challenging, but the unwavering support of Dadi, Dadu, and Papa made it bearable. Dadi prepared healthy, nourishing meals. Dadu managed all the grocery shopping and took you for walks, ensuring you got fresh air and gentle sunlight. Papa and Dadi shared feeding duties, and Papa took over the night shifts.

It was a demanding time, but one filled with immeasurable wonder. Even Oreo, our cat, played a part in welcoming you. He was endlessly curious, staying close to observe you until one of you cried - at which point he'd dash away in surprise! It's a reaction he still has to this day when you're particularly loud.

The days and weeks that followed were difficult for me in ways I'm still processing. But through all the challenges, you two were my constant source of strength and my reason for persevering. You kept the light within me burning bright. Protecting you, caring for you, and loving you with every fiber of my being became my sole focus – my ultimate priority.

I love you, love you, love you, my precious Tara and Dhruv. You are the best parts of me, the greatest adventure I've ever embarked upon, and the most beautiful gift life has given me.

With all my love, always and forever,

Mama

January 14, 2022

Dear Tara and Dhruv,

Wishing you a very Happy Lohri! Primarily in Northern India, we celebrate this popular winter festival to mark new beginnings and the harvest season. It's currently 11:20 a.m., and your Dadi is cradling Tara while I've just finished feeding Dhruv. He's now in my arms, half-asleep and occasionally trying to pass gas—a common occurrence these days. Dealing with colic has proven to be quite a challenge, despite our efforts with probiotics, gas relief drops, and massages. I've even cut down on dairy so that my pumped milk doesn't cause you any issues.

Over the past week, all four of us – Papa, Mama, Dadi, and Dadu – have been actively helping you both burp. It's a bit hectic, especially when you seem calm in our arms but get fussy when we try to put you down. Our backs and shoulders are feeling the strain, but amidst the chaos of feeding, burping, diaper changes, and the relentless quest for your well-being, the love and concern we feel for you are immeasurable.

Though there are moments of frustration in trying to establish our new routine, holding you in my arms as you peacefully sleep brings indescribable comfort. I eagerly await the day when both of you can sleep for longer stretches at night, giving us all some relief. The math of two babies to two parents feels impossible some days – when you both need me simultaneously, I feel torn in half, wishing I could multiply myself. However, I also treasure these precious moments of simply holding you close and witnessing your calm repose.

Today, as we celebrate Lohri, our extended family has showered us with warm wishes. Dadi and Dadu even got Rewari and Gajak (traditional sweets made from sesame seeds and jaggery) from Apna Bazaar, the Indian grocery store in Sunnyvale, California – a place I am always happy to visit. You're fortunate to have such devoted grandparents. Your Nanu and Nani, though unable to visit due to the ongoing global health crisis, miss you dearly. Nani makes it a point to connect through video calls every day, eagerly waiting to see you. They're sending traditional Indian clothes for you, anticipating that you'll look adorable in your first cultural attire.

Dadi, in her excitement, asked today, "What special treats shall we have for Tara and Dhruv on their first Lohri?" Of course, she knew you're far too little for sweets – it's just the way we adults playfully talk to babies, imagining future celebrations. I, speaking on behalf of both of you, heartwarmingly replied, "Lots and lots and lots of kisses." It's moments like these that make all the challenges worthwhile.

As I write this, you're just over a month old. Every day brings new discoveries, challenges, and moments of pure wonder. While the sleepless nights and perpetual care can be exhausting, the happiness you bring to our lives is immeasurable.

With all my love,

Mama

February 10, 2022

Dear Tara and Dhruv,

Putting both of you to bed is quite the process, involving about two hours of feeding, burping, and then finally rocking you to sleep. It's 4:30 a.m., and Dhruv, you're stirring, about to wake up. Your last feed was at 1:30 a.m. These days have been quite demanding for us. Dhruv, you tend to get a bit restless and start squirming, needing us to cradle you before you calm down and fall back asleep – the pacifier comes in handy too. Tara, you have your own way of letting us know you're tired; you start crying, and we gently rock you to sleep. In the end, you both manage to sleep for only half an hour, and we consider ourselves fortunate if it stretches to an hour or if your sleeping schedules happen to coincide.

The hardest part about having twins is that you both need me at exactly the same time. When Dhruv is crying to be fed and Tara needs to be burped, I feel physically torn. There's no taking turns, no "one at a time" - it's both of you, right now, with equal urgency. Some nights I've found myself crying along with you both, feeling utterly defeated by the simple mathematics of two babies and two hands.

Oreo, our furry friend (yes, that's our cat!), has also awakened and is in his playful mood, seemingly having his own witching hour. As I write this, you're both making adorable little grunting sounds, making me wonder if I'll ever finish this sentence. And that's okay—most of our days are filled with unfinished tasks; a partially washed bottle, a shower left incomplete, a dish awaiting cooking, or a message left untyped.

However, amid this chaotic routine, your Papa and I feel incredibly grateful and fortunate to have Dadi and Dadu providing unwavering support. They're helping us navigate through these challenging times, where our primary focus is on feeding you, nourishing ourselves, rocking you to sleep, and grabbing a few precious minutes of rest.

Your Papa takes charge from 11:00 p.m. to about 2:30 a.m., starting to get ready for bed when I wake up at 1:30 a.m. I pump and tend to you until around 6:30 a.m. when Dadi takes over. I take a short rest at 7:00, then wake up at 9:30, pump again, and resume bottle washing and feeding. This schedule sounds organized on paper, but in reality, it's constantly disrupted by your unpredictable needs. Papa starts his day at 8:00, working on some truly fascinating projects in consumer devices. He's currently working on an exciting new product – I can't wait to see how you'll interact with it as you grow older!

Your grandparents continue to shower you with devotion from dawn till dusk, providing us with invaluable assistance. Dadu ensures we have our groceries, and Dadi keeps us well-fed with her delicious cooking. Dadu is aware of my fondness for fenugreek (Methi) curry and ensures its regular availability. He even takes the extra step of personally cleaning the fenugreek leaves for me. This thoughtful gesture reflects the abundant care that surrounds us all. What would we do without them?!

Although I anticipated Dhruv waking up by now, you seem to be enjoying a bit more sleep tonight. Tara, you're still peacefully dreaming too. I initially thought I wouldn't have time for a nap, so I began writing this letter, but it seems you both had other plans, allowing me a little more time to express my thoughts. Witnessing you sleep peacefully brings immense comfort, knowing that you're growing each day.

And as timing would have it, I'm finishing this letter just as Dhruv wakes up. Ciao :-)

With all my love,

Mama

March 30, 2022

Dear Tara and Dhruv,

Hello, my little stars! You're now about three and a half months old, and every day brings new discoveries about your budding personalities and the happiness you bring to our lives.

I find myself in a rare moment of calm amid the delightful chaos that is our daily routine. Dhruv, you're peacefully sleeping beside me in your swing, while Tara, you're engrossed in playtime with Dadi on your new playmat. What makes the playmat even more special is the large mirror that captivates both of you – your reflections have become playful companions in their own right.

Dhruv, you've developed a particular fondness for the toys adorning the playmat – especially the giraffe, which seems to hold a special place in your tiny heart. You also love the elephant, the cloud, and the butterfly. You appear content exploring these wonders on your own. Tara, on the other hand, you find the most delight in the company of others while playing. It's truly fascinating to witness the distinct personalities that you both are developing.

As I jot down these moments, I'm reminded of the recent nights from only a month ago when you'd wake up in the middle of the night, looking at me with your innocent eyes and blessing me with the most heartwarming smiles and laughter. While you're starting to sleep for longer stretches now, I can see how those middle-of-the-night moments were truly magical. When you read this someday, ask me to share those precious videos capturing these special times.

My pumping session has come to an end, and as I conclude this entry, I'm hoping to get a quick shower before Dhruv wakes up, while Tara, you're still happily playing with Dadi. These stolen moments for basic self-care have become precious commodities – I've learned to celebrate even a five-minute uninterrupted shower! We also have an appointment today to notarize your application forms for OCI (Overseas Citizenship of India), another administrative task for immigrant parents. When this process is complete, you'll both be able to travel to India without needing visas – opening up a world of adventures and family connections.

Sending you endless love and hugs,

Your Mama

March 31, 2022

Dear Tara and Dhruv,

Today brought so much happiness to our little family. Both of you tasted banana for the first time and relished it with sheer enthusiasm! Your eyes lit up, and your tiny hands eagerly reached for more. Tara, you found solace in the soothing notes of the song "Nindiya" by Kaavish. Interestingly, the lullaby is sung by Srijata, a senior of mine from my undergrad days. She was known for her beautiful voice and often won singing competitions at our university.

As you're approaching your four-month milestone, I'm eager to arrange another photoshoot to capture this precious stage. We had our first newborn photoshoot when you were about 3 weeks old, and now I want to document how much you've grown. You're both flourishing and growing stronger each day. The sound of your laughter has become the sweetest melody, filling our home with warmth and lifting everyone's spirits.

We've made an unexpected discovery that's turned into a wonderful part of our routine – the "magical" diaper changing station. It's funny how things change; when you were newborns, you both despised being on the changing table, probably because of the cold sensation when we undressed you. But now, it's become a place of pure entertainment! As soon as we lay you down there, you both start chatting, smiling, and even laughing. It's such a charming transformation that Dadi first noticed.

This little trick has been a lifesaver, turning potential tears into smiles and giggles. It's these small, unexpected pleasures that make the journey of parenthood so rewarding. Who would have thought that diaper changes could become a highlight of our day?

Speaking of which, I think I hear some rustling from the nursery. It might be time for another visit to our magical station! I'll sign off for now, but there's always more to share about your adventures.

With all my love,

Mama

April 10, 2022

Dear Tara and Dhruv,

Today, as I watched your papa patiently feeding both of you, singing softly to soothe your fussiness, I was overwhelmed with gratitude. His unwavering dedication reminded me just how fortunate we are, and I felt compelled to share with you just how special your papa is.

You are undoubtedly the luckiest babies in the world to have such a wonderful dad, and I consider myself the luckiest wife to have him as my husband. He is an extraordinary person, and I want you to know the depth of his character.

Your papa is the sweetest soul I know. His words are gentle, his tone is soft, and he carries himself with unwavering respect. The way he treats me with unconditional respect means more to me than anything in the world. He is thoughtful, kind, and stands by me through thick and thin. He is my pillar of strength, always having faith in me. But he is also my weakness – I would go to great lengths for him, and I feel incomplete without him. I cannot fathom my life without the man who brings happiness to every moment and every day.

As a father, your papa is equally remarkable. I've watched him spend countless hours rocking you to sleep, changing diapers with a smile, and reading stories with animated voices that make you both giggle. Just yesterday, he spent the entire afternoon building a pillow fort with you, Tara, while simultaneously helping Dhruv practice sitting up. His calm persistence seems endless, whether he's cleaning up after your messy mealtimes or soothing you during your teething discomfort.

What amazes me most is how he balances his demanding job with being fully present for our family. He never fails to make time for our nightly family walks, where he points out stars and tells you about constellations. During your bath time, he's invented a whole cast of rubber duck characters, each with its own voice and personality, that have you both squealing with excitement.

His love for you both is unparalleled, and it's a treasure that will last a lifetime. The way his eyes light up when he sees you, the tender way he holds you, and the pride in his voice when he talks about you to others - it's all a testament to the depth of his love.

Your papa is truly one of a kind, and I hope as you grow up, you'll cherish and appreciate the incredible person he is. His character is shaping our family in beautiful ways every day.

With all my love,

Your Mom

April 11, 2022

Dear Tara and Dhruv,

Today held several significant milestones for both of you, and I wanted to capture these moments in this letter.

Tara, for the first time, you slept for more than an hour during the day. This might seem small, but for us, it's a huge step forward! Dhruv, you're usually our champion daytime sleeper, but today you seemed to enjoy the quieter house while your sister napped. You were particularly content playing with your toys, babbling happily to yourself. It's these small victories that fill our hearts with hope.

Inspired by Tara's longer nap, we decided to begin sleep training for both of you that same night. The decision wasn't made lightly – until now, you needed constant soothing whenever you stirred. We'd been rocking you back to sleep every half hour, sometimes both of you simultaneously, which was becoming physically and emotionally unsustainable. When Tara showed she had the capacity to sleep longer, we realized it might be time.

Parenting in the social media age makes these decisions even more challenging. One Instagram reel tells you sleep training is essential for your sanity and your babies' development. The next makes you feel like you're failing your crying child. I found myself scrolling through contradictory advice at 3 a.m., questioning every choice.

The first few nights of Ferber's were the hardest of my life. Listening to you cry while fighting every instinct to rush in and comfort you felt like emotional torture. But the physical pain of hearing you cry wasn't the only challenge we faced. Many people around us questioned our approach. "How can you let them cry?" they asked. What made it even more difficult was that while your Papa was equally committed to sleep training – in fact, he was the one who first suggested we try it – somehow I became the focus of most criticism while he remained largely unquestioned. It's fascinating how society often assumes the mother must be making the harsh decisions, even when both parents are in complete agreement.

But after about a week of consistency, something beautiful happened. With a darkened room, the comforting hum of white noise, and snug swaddles, you both learned to self-soothe. The transformation felt like magic – you slept so peacefully, offering us a sigh of relief and a glimpse into the promise of restful nights ahead.

However, the sleep milestone wasn't the most significant event today. This morning, you both received your scheduled vaccinations. The pain and tears that followed were heart-wrenching. Tara, you seemed especially affected, crying persistently. Dhruv, while you were quieter, your little furrowed brow spoke volumes. Witnessing you both in discomfort squeezed my heart, and I found myself wishing I could bear the pain on your behalf.

But your resilience amazed me. After the initial tears and cuddles, you both calmed down. Tara, you found comfort in your favorite stuffed elephant, clutching it tightly as you drifted off to sleep. Dhruv, you bounced back quickly, giving us a toothless grin as you played with your rattles.

As your mom, my greatest wish is to shield you from pain, but I know that facing these challenges is a part of growing up. Sometimes the hardest part isn't your pain - it's making decisions that feel right for our family while navigating different opinions. You are both brave and loved beyond measure. Today was a mix of progress and temporary setbacks, but it showed me once again how resilient and adaptable you both are.

With all my love,

Your Mom

May 12, 2022

Dear Tara and Dhruv,

Today was a day filled with the sweet melody of your laughter as you played with your piano play mat. Both of you were so animated, creating music in your own wonderful ways. Dhruv, you used your little hands to explore the notes with methodical curiosity, while Tara, you danced to the tunes with your tiny feet, swaying with an instinct that seems to come from somewhere deep within.

Watching you both respond to music fills me with such profound happiness. It takes me back to my own childhood, when the sound of ghungroo – the small ankle bells worn in Indian classical dance – jingling with each step was my greatest comfort. Dance and music were my escape, my stress relief, my way of expressing what words couldn't capture. I spent years learning Kathak, losing myself in the intricate footwork and graceful movements. At Indraprastha College for Women in Delhi University, I was part of the classical music society, and we'd travel to other colleges to perform and compete. Those moments on stage, sharing our culture through song and dance, shaped who I am.

Music runs deeper in our family than you might know. Mataji, my dadi, used to sing Shabad Kirtan at gurudwaras in pre-independence India and Bangladesh. Even then, as a young woman in a time when opportunities for women were limited, she found her voice through devotional music. That same spirit, that same connection to rhythm and melody, flows through our bloodline.

But raising twins means I rarely get those peaceful moments to simply enjoy your musical discoveries. Just as Tara finds her rhythm, Dhruv needs attention. When Dhruv is focused on creating his little piano masterpiece, Tara wants to dance but ends up disrupting his concentration. I find myself constantly managing two different musical moods, two different needs for creative expression. Sometimes I wonder if single children get to fully immerse themselves in activities like this, with their parents' undivided attention to appreciate every note, every movement – and I'll admit, the thought comes with frustration and even a touch of jealousy.

Yet even amidst this chaos, there are fleeting moments when everything aligns perfectly. The sheer wonder in your eyes when you look at me and your Papa, discover a new book, or encounter a new toy is absolutely mesmerizing. Each moment is a treasure, and your happiness fills our hearts with such warmth. Your playful spirits bring light to our days, and we treasure every little melody you create.

These glimpses of watching you learn and grow are what make parenthood so rewarding, even when they're interrupted and fragmented. The music you make isn't just from the piano mat – it's the sound of your giggles, the patter of your feet, and the babbles of your own secret language. It's a symphony that only a parent's heart can truly appreciate, even when it's competing with the beautiful mayhem of managing two little musicians at once.

I dream of the day when I can teach you both the dances I learned, when we can move together to classical ragas or Punjabi folk songs. I imagine Tara's natural rhythm developing into something beautiful, and Dhruv's methodical approach to the piano keys evolving into real musicianship. Maybe music will be your stress reliever too, the way those ghungroos were mine.

As you continue to explore and discover, know that your Papa and I will always be your biggest fans, cheering you on at every step. Your curiosity and zest for life inspire us daily. Keep making your beautiful music, my little ones.

With all my love,

Mama

July 4, 2022

My Dearest Tara and Dhruv,

Happy Independence Day! Today marks a day of fireworks, a spectacle you'll one day be big enough to appreciate. People paint the sky with their beauty, creating a magical atmosphere that I can't wait to share with you when you're older.

At approximately seven months old, you both radiate beauty in your own unique ways. Dhruv, your mischievous charm continues to shine through, and your fascination with toys remains as strong as ever. Your curiosity and excitement during playtime are contagious, spreading warmth to everyone around you. Witnessing your enthusiasm as you move from one corner to another, exploring each toy, lights up our faces with pure happiness.

Tara, you still find your greatest satisfaction in being with other people, especially Papa. The bond you share is evident in the smiles you exchange - it's truly heartwarming to witness. You've been working hard on your physical development too. When attempting to crawl, you often end up striking a boat pose—looking like a little superhero ready to soar high like a bird. Remarkably, you've also started sitting up, a testament to all the yoga boat poses you've been practicing.

Dhruv, you were the first to roll over, and we celebrated

that milestone with such pride. Each of you is reaching developmental markers at your own pace, and we celebrate every achievement, big or small.

Your unique personalities continually amaze Papa and me. You two bring immense happiness to our lives and, truth be told, a fair share of exhaustion too. But your hugs warm and energize my heart, and the innocent, loving gaze you share speaks volumes. That smile, conveying that Papa and I mean the world to you, is a common thread between you two, despite the differences in your personalities and preferences.

As we celebrate this day of independence, I'm reminded of the freedom we do have and how grateful we are to be on this journey with the both of you. Your presence has given new meaning to everything we do, and I cannot imagine it being any other way.

I adore you both dearly,

Your Mom

July 17, 2022

Dear Tara and Dhruv,

I hope this letter finds you well and brings you the warmth of our devotion and blessings. As I write to you both, my heart is heavy with the struggles and disappointments we have faced as a family since moving to this foreign land we now call home.

The recent overturning of Roe v. Wade has cast a shadow on the promise of a brighter future that I envisioned for you in the United States. It's disheartening to witness a society that, in many ways, fails to live up to the ideals I had hoped for. From the anti-immigration policies enacted during Donald Trump's presidency, to the instability and isolation of the COVID-19 pandemic, and now to the erosion of reproductive rights following the Supreme Court's reversal of Roe v. Wade, we have weathered storms that tested our resilience as a family.

To begin with, the uncertainties surrounding travel bans and restrictive policies during the pandemic added a new type of stress to our lives. As I pursued my PhD at the University of Texas at Austin's LBJ School of Public Affairs (I'm now nearing the end of my fourth year), being asked to leave the country if classes went remote was a stark reminder of our outsider status. This threat loomed over us, adding to the already demanding task of balancing academic pursuits with starting a family in a foreign land. Your Papa and I got married amidst these obstacles, unable to have our loved ones present, except for your Dadi. Later, when I was pregnant with both of you, visa appointment delays prevented Nani and Nanu from being with us during those vulnerable times.

Moving from Boston to California during the early stages of my pregnancy presented its own set of difficulties. Balancing health insurance and caring for you and myself while working on my dissertation proposal required a strength I didn't know I possessed. Fortunately, your Dadi and Dadu managed to arrive in time for your birth. Their hard work and sacrifices played a crucial role in keeping both of you and me healthy, showing just how boundless their devotion for you both is.

In hindsight though, I wonder if even having my parents here would have provided the support I was imagining. As first-generation immigrants, our parents depend on us for everything - from getting groceries to understanding how systems work. They have no friends here, no familiar rhythms of daily life, no community built over decades. America's car-dependent economy traps them in ways they never were back home, where they could walk to the market or take a rickshaw to the temple. Here, they cannot leave the house unless one of us drives them. Their isolation, both physical and emotional, takes an enormous toll.

Beyond that, generational differences in parenting are inevitable and challenging for everyone involved. We're trying to parent differently in some ways - shaped by different research, different cultural context, different pressures - and our parents are trying to help using the wisdom they know. When these approaches don't align, it creates tender moments where everyone feels a bit misunderstood, adding emotional complexity to an already demanding time.

Raising twins while managing my own emotional needs felt impossible some days, and I desperately needed someone who could understand my exhaustion without judgment. But perhaps that's a fantasy - the idea that anyone, even our own mothers, could fully meet us in this particular American immigrant experience of early (or even late?) parenthood.

The healthcare in the U.S is commendable, but the toll on my mental health during these last two years has been undeniable, and the recent overturning of Roe v. Wade only adds to my concerns about the society in which you are growing up. The patriarchy and discrimination against women, which I hoped to leave behind in India, seem to have found new expression here.

I regret that you were born into a society where women are not treated fairly. The ban on abortions reflects a society that values the unborn but does not prioritize the well-being of women facing dangerous pregnancies. It pains me that the emphasis of 'life' is solely on a baby's birth, but then it is acceptable for them to suffer due to a lack of resources. The privilege enjoyed by men in this society, allowing them to play with the lives of women without accountability, is a stark contrast to the struggles and expectations placed on women.

Tara, remember that your family stands with you through thick and thin. Whenever you feel discriminated against, come back home to us. Your mom, Papa, Dadu, Dadi, Nanu, Nani, Tayaji, Tayiji, and Mamu are wonderful individuals who will always support you. We will listen, care for you, and find solutions to any problem together. And Dhruv, use your privilege wisely. Respect and appreciate women for the remarkable roles they play in your life. A woman has given you a part of her body and her entire heart, and your sister adores you unconditionally, sharing both your happiness and sorrows.

Though society may not be perfect, let us endeavor to cultivate moments of affection, honor, and respect within our family, transcending the boundaries of any country we reside in. I hope you both grow up to be advocates for equality and justice, always standing up for what's right.

With all my devotion and blessings,

Your Mom

July 18, 2022

Dear Tara and Dhruv,

On this wonderful day, a significant milestone was reached in our household—Tara, at only eight months old, you spoke your first words! It was a heartwarming moment that I must capture and share with both of you.

It happened in the early evening, just as I was preparing dinner. Tara, you were sitting in your high chair, watching me intently as I moved around the kitchen. Suddenly, the air was filled with the first echoes of "Amma," "Amma," and "Amma." Since Amma means "mother" in many Indian languages, that is the term your Papa uses for me in your presence. It seemed only natural that this would be what you called me.

Tara, your words marked your acknowledgment of my role in your life. The feeling was unique, not easily described— neither mere excitement nor overwhelming emotions. Instead, it was a blend of pride, warmth, affection, and an indescribable something that touched the very core of my being.

Knowing that you chose to say "Amma" first instills a sense of pride and elation within me. It feels like a recognition of the significant role I play in your world—a silent but powerful acknowledgment of gratitude. A subtle "thank you" for enduring the difficulties of pregnancy, battling through preeclampsia, cholestasis, and various other medical hurdles. A thank you for bringing you both into this world against all odds. Thank you for the countless hours spent pumping milk, sacrificing personal freedom, and early mornings to feed and play with you. Thank you for providing you with the best toys, books, and gadgets we could. Thank you for temporarily putting aside my career and dreams to nurture yours. Thank you for smiling and playing with you even during moments of personal struggle.

There's something bittersweet about twin milestones - the pure happiness of witnessing your growth, Tara, mixed with a tiny ache wondering when Dhruv will reach this same moment. With twins, every "first" becomes a reminder that you're two separate little people developing at your own pace. I find myself celebrating your achievement while silently hoping Dhruv doesn't feel left behind, even though at seven months, he has no concept of being "second."

Tara, your words are more than just sounds—they are a heartfelt expression of connection and gratitude. Dhruv, while you haven't spoken your first word yet, I know it's coming soon, and I'm equally excited to hear what you'll say.

Your Papa and I, in turn, want you both to know how much we adore you, appreciate you, and are grateful for everything you bring to our lives. I cherish you dearly—more than words can express.

With all my devotion,

Your Amma

December 20, 2022

Dear Tara and Dhruv,

We are moving in a few days from our current home in Mountain View, California to Milpitas, California for a bigger house and a daycare for you. As we bid farewell to this two-bedroom apartment where we've resided for the past year, I can't help but reflect on the beautiful memories we've created here. Although I know that as you grow, you will have houses of your own, for now, every place we stay is transformed into a lovely home—filled with the wonder and (yes, sometimes) weariness of having you in our lives.

Watching you both grow and witnessing your distinct personalities emerging is a genuine treat. Recently, we celebrated your first birthday with not one, not two, but three parties! The first was a few days before your birthday, and the second was the day after your birthday. You might wonder why we didn't celebrate on the actual date, and the answer is simple—friends.

Shriya, Ravi, Samir, and Mira have been pillars of support since your birth. They were there at the hospital, delivering food, babysitting, and showering us with care. Ravi and Shriya were leaving for India on your actual birthday, so we celebrated early. Samir and Mira, eagerly awaiting their baby girl, had their baby shower on your birthday. We didn't want to miss their celebration, and they didn't want to miss yours. To our surprise and happiness, they surprised us with a special cake for you during their shower—hence, three parties!

Your Dadu and Dadi traveled all the way from India to celebrate with us. Dadi baked special cupcakes for you without sugar, using almond flour, yogurt, banana, and strawberries—a treat you both devoured eagerly. They also brought Indian outfits that made you look absolutely dazzling at all three celebrations!

Lately, you've both taken to using the walker, and it won't be long before you're walking on your own. It's adorable to watch, but I must admit, it's quite exhausting for us. We're constantly on our toes, trying to protect you from falls, head bumps, and the occasional taste of sand throughout the day. Managing two mobile babies means we're always outnumbered - one of you heads toward the stairs while the other discovers Oreo's food bowl. It's like a constant game of zone defense that we're slowly learning to master.

As we prepare for this move, I'm filled with a mix of emotions. There's excitement for our new home and the memories we'll create there, but also a touch of nostalgia for this place where we became a family. Every corner of this apartment holds a precious memory—your first smiles, first words, first steps with the walker. We're not just packing boxes; we're wrapping up a chapter of our lives.

The logistics of moving with twins feels overwhelming - double the baby gear, double the comfort items that can't be packed until the last minute, double the anxiety about disrupting your routines. But I'm also grateful we're moving to a place with more space for you to explore and grow.

I look forward to seeing how you'll explore our new home, which new corners will become your favorite play spots, and what new adventures await us there. Change can be challenging, but with you two, every day is an exciting new journey.

Lots of affection,

Your Mama

April 27, 2023

Dear Tara and Dhruv,

Greetings from 30,000 feet above, cruising on a flight from Delhi to Bagdogra. I traveled to Delhi for my student visa stamping appointment[2] a couple of days ago, leaving you in the loving care of your Nani and Nanu. From the photos and video updates I've been receiving, they are taking exceptional care of you. Under your Nani's care, you've been enjoying nutritious meals, playing gleefully with Nanu, and seemingly relishing your oil massages.

Your first journey to India began on March 27, 2023 – your inaugural visit to this vibrant country. The three of us embarked on this adventure, traversing the skies like absolute champions. Papa stayed back in California since he had limited vacation time, and honestly, I desperately needed this extended time "home." I was struggling with postpartum feelings and craved the comfort of familiar surroundings and my mother's care.

---

[2] The U.S. student visa is commonly referred to as the "F-1 visa." While I did have this visa, it must be renewed periodically (typically every five years). The renewal process required traveling back to my home country and obtaining a new visa stamp from the U.S. Embassy in India before being permitted to re-enter the United States.

While I wouldn't recommend undertaking a 24-hour international flight solo with two 15-month-old twins, you both handled it better than I expected – though it was still exhausting. The hardest part wasn't the crying or the diaper changes at 35,000 feet – it was the looks from other passengers when you both had meltdowns simultaneously. There's something uniquely overwhelming about managing two toddlers' needs while feeling judged by strangers in a confined space.

Upon our arrival in Delhi, both of you were battling fevers, colds, and severe jet lag. Nani met us there, and we stayed overnight at one of the Aerocity hotels before flying to Bagdogra the next day. During that difficult stretch, she became my anchor — washing and sterilizing every bottle, holding you in her arms for hours, and quietly taking over so I could breathe for a moment. That small relief meant more than I can explain.

After the two-hour flight to Bagdogra and a short car ride to Siliguri, you finally fell into a deep sleep in our arms for over six hours. Your Choti nani and Badi nani came to see you that first day, but the exhaustion from the long journey left you barely able to open your eyes.

As the days unfolded, and after overcoming two bouts of viral fevers, you've come to love the comforts of your grandparents' house. It's fascinating to observe your growth, witnessing the emergence of distinct choices and preferences. As always, Dhruv finds happiness in playing with his toys, but now both of you enjoy the playful ritual of taking items like cloth clips and hair clips, placing them in a box, and then taking them out again. Tara has also become remarkably aware of the ownership of things in the house. For instance, she insists on her hat before a walk and points and vocalizes if we forget. Once the hat is on, she lets out a satisfied "Aaah." She eagerly brings me my shoes before an outing, insists on her favorite jacket, and even guards my jewelry from being shared, not even with Nani.

As another new development, Dhruv has embraced a mischievous side. His adventures include balcony escapades, throwing cloth pins from our third-floor balcony to the park below, excavating soil from house plants, indulging in a bit of soil-tasting, and then spreading it across the floor. These moments are crowned with a quirky smile, a silent acknowledgment of his naughtiness.

Lakkhi didi, an integral part of our family for over sixteen years now, has been wonderful with you both during this first meeting. As our domestic help whom we all cherish like family, she's taken to you immediately. She gifted you two silver bangles that look so beautiful on you.

While everyone, including Nani, Nanu, big Nani, and Lakkhi didi, feel the strains in their shoulders, wrists, and waists from holding you, the constant naughtiness, beautiful smiles, and happy faces keep us all going. You are our adorable bundles of wonder, and we adore you to the core, always praying for your happiness and health.

Sending heaps of affection,

Your Mom

September 19, 2023

Dear Tara and Dhruv,

My sweet babies, let me share some of the wonderful things you do these days.

1. Your fascination with animals has grown so much recently. You both imitate a wolf's howl, filling our home with playful sounds. Tara's animated reactions to the book "Moo, Baa, La La La" by Sandra Boynton are absolutely precious - your giggles and attempts to mimic the animal sounds make story time magical. And Dhruv, you especially impress us with your knowledge of animals. If we focus on tigers in one book, you gather all the books featuring tigers, open them to the respective pages, and enthusiastically exclaim, "ti, ti, ti." You even fetch the tiger bath toy! "Tortoise" is particularly adorable when you say "Torto" in your sweet little voices.

2. I love both of your dance moves to "Baby Shark," "Wheels on the Bus," "Itsy Bitsy Spider," and "Head, Shoulders, Knees, and Toes." Your enthusiasm for these songs never fails to bring smiles to our faces, though getting you both to dance the same song at the same time is like herding

cats!

3. Tara has a sassy way of saying "Yeah" and "No," showing remarkable determination at such a young age. Your confidence in making choices is truly endearing, even when you're being defiant about wearing shoes.

4. Dhruv exhibits remarkable independence, insisting on feeding himself with a spoon and engaging in solitary play until he figures out his toys. Your meticulous nature shines through in these moments, though it means meal times take twice as long.

5. "Cow" seems to be Dhruv's favorite word right now. When I asked your name one day, you confidently replied, "Cow." It often comes out as your first word in the morning, which never fails to make us chuckle.

6. Tara engages in babbling that sounds like complete sentences, as if having serious conversations. Your charming smiles and a cheerful "Hi" whenever you look at me, Papa, or any of your dear ones brighten our days.

7. You've both mastered the art of synchronized mischief – when one of you discovers something you shouldn't touch, you immediately alert the other, and suddenly I'm dealing with two little explorers getting into trouble together.

8. Your bedtime routine has become a negotiation process where Tara insists on three stories while Dhruv demands to arrange all his cars in a perfect line before sleep. Somehow, you both manage to coordinate these demands perfectly.

Watching you both grow and develop your unique personalities is a constant source of joy and wonder for us. Each day brings new surprises and adventures, and we treasure every moment of this journey with you, chaos and all.

Love, love, love,

Your Mom

September 19, 2023

Dear Tara and Dhruv,

I must share with you the events of last night. Tara, you woke up in tears, distressed by pain in your legs, likely stemming from lingering effects of your recent Roseola virus infection. We tried various methods to soothe your discomfort - gentle massages, soft lullabies, and even your favorite stuffed toy - but you continued crying. After half an hour together in the living room, where I massaged your legs, I returned you to your crib. However, your cries persisted, and your distress woke Dhruv from his sleep. So far, he had managed to avoid getting sick.

The reality of having twins is that we can't truly isolate one of you when the other is sick — it's simply impossible in our small space with two curious toddlers who share everything. This has been our ongoing struggle since birth, through countless illnesses — pneumonia, the flu, Norovirus, RSV, and several rounds of the mysterious "guess what now?" sickness. Often, we end up with two sick children simultaneously, and some-times the illness spreads to Papa and me too. There's nothing quite like trying to care for two fever-ridden toddlers while battling the same virus yourself. Desperately trying to keep everyone hydrated and nourished while feeling utterly depleted. I dread these times with a bone-deep exhaustion. The dread starts the moment one of you shows the first symptom, knowing what's coming. But they're an unavoidable part of our twin journey and the only way to move forward is to accept our realities.

Coming back to the events of last night—in response to your continued distress, Papa and I moved the mattress from the guest bedroom to your room so we could be close to you both. Taking both of you out of your cribs, we attempted to rest on the floor mattress. Dhruv, you quickly fell back asleep, but Tara, you were unwilling to settle. Eventually, your tears subsided, replaced by a sudden burst of energy. You began bouncing on the mattress, playfully pulling my hair and even pinching my nose, followed by Dhruv's nose and ears while he was still peacefully asleep. After a while, I placed you back in your crib, where you cried briefly before finally succumbing to sleep, but not before the commotion woke Dhruv up. He began his own nighttime adventure, managing to open the door (when did he learn to do that?) and venturing out of the room while Papa and I were momentarily distracted by Tara's settling.

Dhruv sprinted out of the room and then returned to the bedroom, playfully touching the mattress, then me, before darting back out again. Despite my weariness, it was endearing to witness this little game of tag. At one point, when Dhruv was gone for over a minute, I stepped out to find a tiny silhouette in the living room, engrossed in a book in the darkness — another heartwarming sight.

Even at three in the morning, books seemed to call to him. I've always believed that a love for reading is one of the greatest gifts a child can nurture — it builds imagination, empathy, curiosity, and a quiet companionship that lasts a lifetime. Books become friends, teachers, and windows into worlds far beyond our own.

Still, I couldn't help but wonder — what exactly was he reading in the dark? A thrilling mystery? A manual on toddler independence? Or perhaps he was simply "reading" the pictures and creating his own grand story.

However, the need for rest prevailed. It was 3 a.m., and fatigue weighed heavily upon us. Eventually, we settled Dhruv back into his crib, and he, too, drifted into sleep.

It was an eventful night, and we all awoke at 9 am the next morning, hastily preparing you for daycare. By then, Tara was past the contagious stage, though with twins, these distinctions often feel meaningless. As I write this, I'm exhausted but smiling. These challenging nights are part of our journey together, and I know that as time passes, the memories of your midnight antics and those precious moments of seeing you engrossed in play or books, even in the wee hours, will far outweigh the fatigue we felt. Every day with you two is an adventure, even (or especially) in the middle of the night. I don't want to endure them because they're exhausting and feel horrible in the moment—but like everyone says, they pass really soon.

All my love,

Your Mom

September 20, 2023

Dear Tara and Dhruv,

Today marked a sweet milestone in your lives - at almost two years old, you had ice cream popsicles for the first time!

Tara, your reaction was absolutely priceless. As soon as the cold popsicle touched your lips, your eyes widened with surprise. Then, as the sweetness hit your taste buds, a huge grin spread across your face. You started giggling and bouncing in your high chair, making excited "Mmm!" sounds between licks. Your enthusiasm was contagious, and soon we were all laughing along with you.

Dhruv, always my little problem solver, you approached this new treat with your typical thoughtfulness. Instead of diving right in, you studied the popsicle for a moment, then reached for your spoon. Your determination to eat the melting ice cream with a utensil was utterly adorable. Even as it dripped down your hands and arms, you persisted with the spoon, occasionally looking up at us with a proud smile.

Managing two toddlers with their first popsicles was quite the adventure—sticky hands everywhere, dripping treats, and the inevitable need for immediate cleanup before the mess spread everywhere. But watching your completely different approaches to the same new experience reminded me how wonderfully unique you both are.

I wanted to capture this precious memory, so I took a video of the experience, and I can't wait to watch it back with you when you're older. I'm sure we'll share plenty of laughs over Tara's excited bouncing and Dhruv's spoon technique!

These little moments of discovery are what make parenting so rewarding. Watching you experience new things and develop your own unique approaches to the world fills my heart with warmth and pride.

Here's to many more sweet firsts in your lives!

All my love,

Mom

October 22, 2023

Dear Tara and Dhruv,

As you embrace the wonders of the world around you, I can't help but marvel at your rapidly expanding vocabulary at 23 months. You're learning both English and our home languages – Hindi and Punjabi are naturally woven into your daily vocabulary. Here's a snapshot of the incredible words and concepts you've embraced:

Body Parts:

- Head · Eyes · Ears · Nose · Heart · Hand · Toes · Mouth · Cheek · Knees · Teeth · Arms · Lips

Animals (with their sounds when you make them, or how you say their names):

- Cow (Moo) · Sheep (Baa) · Dog (Bhow Bhow) · Lion (Roar) · Duck (Quack) · Tiger (Ti) · Cat (Meow) · Giraffe · Bird · Tortoise (Torto) · Fish · Owl (Hoot Hoot) · Bear · Bee · Mouse · Goat (Baa) · Snail · Rhino · Bunny · Elephant (E) · Snake (Hiss) · Squirrel (Quirrel) · Hippo · Seal (Ou Ou Ou) · Monkey (Oo Oo Aa Aa)

Everything Else:

- More · La La La · Hi · Bye · Yeah · No · Wawa (Water) · Ball · Car · Star · Moon · Bag · Mama · Papa · Book · Airplane · Dada (for Ms. Rachel) · Eat · Hat · Ne Ne (for shoes) · I Love You · Park · Go · Bahar (Outside) · Yum · Baby · Poo Poo · Aa (for Aaradh) · Astro · Dadi · Square · This · Dadu · Boat · In · Circle · Up · Down · Egg · Chachu · Nani · Nanu · Oreo · Chair · Milk · Dude · Bucket · Toys · Blocks · Open · Close · Help · Slide · Night Night · Annie (friend from daycare) · Rainbow · Not Now Cow · No No Oreo · Oreo Go Bahar · No No Aa · All Done · Mum (Water) · Spoon · Socks · Purple · Coin · Town · Hahaha · Sleep · Wain Wain (Crying) · Nai Nai (Bath) · Sit · Apple · Tree · Walk · Cup · Hot · Banana · One · Two · Three · Four · Five · Ten · Flower · Hug · Kiss · Tug · Slowly · Beep Beep

Your ability to grasp and articulate so many words is remarkable. Each word is a testament to your growing curiosity and the wonderful uniqueness that makes you, you. I'm so proud to have documented every single one. These words represent such precious milestones in your growth.

It's fascinating to see how your vocabulary reflects both our daily life and your individual interests. You both show such curiosity about animals. You've mastered so many creature names and sounds, and your enthusiasm for books about tigers and tortoises is endless. Your shared fascination with movement and transportation comes through in words like "car," "airplane," and "beep beep," and I love watching you discover new things together.

I'm touched by the words that show your emotional growth—

"hug," "kiss," and "I boo boo" are precious additions to your vocabulary. It's amusing to see how you've adapted words like "bahar" (outside) and "nai nai" (bath) from our cultural background. What's especially sweet is that somewhere along the way, you both switched from calling me "Amma" to "Mama"—I didn't even notice when it happened!

Your growing ability to communicate opens up a whole new world of interaction between us. I cherish hearing your thoughts, preferences, and observations, even if they're sometimes expressed in creative combinations of these words!

Language is a powerful tool, my dear ones. As you continue to learn and grow, I hope you'll use your words to express yourselves, to show kindness, and to explore the vast, wonderful world around you.

With much pride and affection,

Mom

November 5, 2023

Dear Tara and Dhruv,

As you become more independent, you continue to melt our hearts—understanding the sentiment behind "I love you" and responding with your adorable "I bo boo" is enchanting. Watching you grow into distinct personalities is mesmerizing.

Your personalities shine through in the most delightful ways. Tara, your sassiness has become legendary in our household. When you don't get your way, you plant your feet firmly, cross your arms, and declare "Oh, no!" with such dramatic flair that we can't help but smile. Just yesterday, when I tried to put on your purple shirt instead of the pink one you wanted, you shook your head vigorously and announced "No no no!" before marching over to the drawer and pointing insistently at your choice. And Dhruv, you've developed quite the mischievous streak. Your latest adventure involved systematically removing all the books from the shelf, creating a mountain in the middle of the living room, and then sitting atop your literary throne with the proudest grin. When I discovered your handiwork, you looked up at me with those twinkling eyes and simply said "Book!" as if that explained everything. These moments of personality—Tara's determination and Dhruv's playful rebellion—remind me daily that you're becoming your own little people.

Every morning follows a wonderful routine as I get you both dressed for the day. Tara, you request your Bhow Bhow (the big gray cat stuffed toy from your Deep Uncle), your bunny (rabbit stuffed toy), and your small Bhow Bhow (the petite orange cat gifted by Raj uncle). Yes, you call both cats and dogs "Bhow Bhow" - it's your universal term for furry animals! I arrange these toys on the floor mattress, with the big Bhow Bhow serving as a pillow and Bunny and the small Bhow Bhow on the sides. You settle on your Bhow Bhow, wrapped in your favorite red and white blanket, eagerly awaiting your morning bottle.

Dhruv, it's your turn next. I arrange your baby shark and penguin (Barfi) as makeshift pillows, though you're not as particular about soft toys—you just need a few favorites. You have quite the attachment to your beloved cars and trucks, especially the garbage truck, ambulance, and bulldozer. You often sleep with them, and occasionally, we hear the cheerful babbling and play sounds emanating from your crib as you discover your favorite vehicles in the middle of the night! When morning arrives, your wake-up signal is the deliberate toss of a truck on the floor, indicating you're up.

Returning to our morning routine, I place Tara down first, followed by Dhruv. While you enjoy your milk, I swiftly dress you both. Sometimes I watch other parents holding their single child in their lap during feeding time, gazing lovingly into their eyes, sharing that intimate bonding moment, and I feel a pang of longing. With twins, I've had to devise strategies to ensure you both get your milk simultaneously - making sure neither of you feels less loved or less attended to. But in optimizing for fairness and efficiency, I realize I've missed out on those quiet, tender moments of simply holding my child and watching them drink, of being fully present in that simple act of nourishment. Instead, my mind is always calculating - who needs what, how to manage both your needs at once, how to make sure I'm being equitable in my attention.

Dhruv's dressing routine is a race—will he finish his bottle before or after I put on his socks? Some mornings, if he finishes his bottle quickly, he's eager to play rather than get dressed. So he might end up in just his diaper for a bit. Once Dhruv is dressed, he dashes outside the room to meet Papa or engage in play. Tara, you patiently wait until Dhruv is ready before I dress you. Your dressing time is more leisurely—no competition here! Once dressed, you share a hug with Papa, and our day unfolds with warmth, laughter, and deep satisfaction as we witness your remarkable growth.

Love, love, love,

Mom

P.S. - As I type out this letter on March 5, 2024, I'm amazed at how things have changed. Now it's Tara who needs to be dressed first thing in the morning. She's become quite particular about her outfits and gets upset if she's not dressed right away. Meanwhile, Dhruv has become more patient, happily waiting for his turn. It's a reminder of how quickly you both grow and change, always keeping us on our toes.

November 18, 2023

Dear Tara and Dhruv,

Today, I want to share a special letter that your Papa wrote about our recent Halloween adventures and other family outings. It's wonderful to see these experiences through his eyes, and I hope you'll treasure his perspective as much as I do.

[Papa's letter begins]

My dearest Tara and Dhruv,

A few days ago, we participated in a Halloween event at Cordoza Park in Milpitas with a Baby Shark theme. We dressed up as family members from the Baby Shark song, and your charming dances to Halloween music, your little legs exploring every nook and cranny, and your enthusiastic greetings to everyone made the event memorable. Although we didn't win the costume contest, our cute shark family garnered many "awws" from onlookers.

We recently made our third visit to Gilroy Gardens for an early Halloween celebration. Dhruv, you stole the show dressed as Buzz Lightyear from Toy Story, radiating cuteness. Our attempt to dress Tara as Woody hit a snag when she insisted on keeping her favorite pink hoodie on, wearing only the bottom part of the costume. Tara, you're quite particular about your preferences.

Our Halloween adventure at Gilroy Gardens was equally wonderful. You both love the theme park and its rides, especially the ones you can ride independently. The fire truck, racer car, goldfish, spinning cups, and the carousel were your favorites. Dhruv, your excitement during the spinning cups ride and Tara, your premature cheers before each ride is over never fail to bring us happiness. Tara, you were especially fond of waving to the passing train.

Dhruv, your mischievous antics have reached new heights. Recently, you nearly leapt off the stairs while we were getting food, and your penchant for climbing railings or dashing down paths keeps us vigilant. During one of our outings, both of you showed your affection for animals by attempting to feed a kitten.

We treasure special moments like Sam's first birthday party (he's the son of Papa's colleague). Dhruv, your enthusiasm during a game of Musical Chairs was unforgettable. Your laughter and clapping when we secured a chair brought delight to everyone. Playing with balloons was another highlight, although Tara found the occasional burst a bit startling.

Taking you to the zoo or farm brings us great pleasure. Witnessing your excitement while interacting with animals, feeding goats or chickens, and exploring enclosures for jaguars, crocodiles, tortoises, and lemurs—it all fills our hearts.

Despite the occasional tiredness and tantrums, seeing you both revel in these experiences makes our days and nights full of warmth and contentment.

Mummy and I treasure every moment with you and adore you endlessly.

Love you, love you, love you,

Papa

[Papa's letter ends]

Reading Papa's letter fills me with such warmth. It's beautiful to see how he captures these precious moments and the happiness you bring to our lives. I'm grateful for the wonderful father he is and how he treasures these experiences with you both.

His words remind me of the importance of seeing the world through your eyes—the excitement, the wonder, and even the occasional stubbornness that makes you uniquely you.

Thank you, my darlings, for making our family adventures so special. And thank you, Papa, for capturing these moments so beautifully.

Love always,

Mama

December 10, 2023

Dear Tara and Dhruv,

You just turned two, and I want to capture the magic of this birthday weekend before the memories fade.

Let me start from Friday—my birthday. I usually visit the Gurdwara to mark the occasion, but this time we went on Saturday morning instead.

The moment we stepped inside, your playful spirits took over. You ran around with shoes still on, touched every decoration within reach, and Dhruv, in a burst of fearless curiosity, even tried to handle the ceremonial sword. Tara, in your own bliss, you circled the Guru Granth Sahib with spirited screams. The langar hall witnessed flying paper plates and tissues, and then came the stair adventure — up and down, again and again. I followed you both three times, heart racing each time you moved too fast or too close to something sharp or sacred.

On paper, when I read this now, it sounds like an adventure. And maybe one day it will feel only that way.

But in that moment, it filled me with anxiety.

I could not sit still and listen to the shabad kirtan. I could not take even one bite of langar without scanning the room to make sure you weren't climbing the stairs again. My body was in constant vigilance — alert, tense, anticipating the next move. And then there were the looks from people around us — some amused, some disapproving. I felt exposed, judged, overwhelmed.

This constant state of alertness when you both explore does not stay only in my thoughts; it lives in my body. A tight chest. A clenched jaw. A nervous system that doesn't fully settle, even after we leave.

There are honest moments when I wish you would just listen. Just sit. Just behave.

But I have been a child once too.

I have been the impulsive, curious child — and more often than not, my parents reacted impulsively in return. With yelling. With shaming. Sometimes with a beating meant to "correct" me. My mind and body still remember those moments. The fear. The shrinking. The silence that followed.

And I could never, ever do that to you.

Yes, I get frustrated. On the very hard days, I make a fist, close my eyes, and take deep breaths. I remind myself of the innocent souls you are. I remind myself of your age — that this is what two-year-olds do. You explore. You test. You move. You ask. And if I shut you down today, you might grow into someone like me — afraid to ask questions, overthinking before disagreeing, carrying frustration in quiet, unhealthy ways.

You do not deserve the burdens I carry. You deserve a present mother — not a perfect one, but one who knows her limitations and works on them. I am doing that work for you. So that you can live freely and confidently. So that you know your place in this world. So that no one can tell you who you are allowed to be.

The rest of Saturday was a whirlwind—a park visit, home for your nap and a cleaning spree, then a friend's birthday party, another park visit, and a quick stop at the dollar store for your birthday decorations. By nightfall, the fatigue was palpable for all of us. I felt physically drained, yet emotionally full. Despite my exhaustion, there was an undercurrent of anticipation knowing that tomorrow would be your special day—a day we'd been looking forward to for weeks. We slept with lingering excitement, bracing ourselves for your big day.

Sunday morning arrived—your second birthday! You woke up to birthday decorations everywhere, and your smiles and gleaming eyes filled the room with pure happiness. Opting out of another Gurdwara visit (after Saturday's escapades!), we headed to our favorite diner for a hearty breakfast of eggs, pancakes, hash browns, and orange juice. Unfortunately, my headache prompted me to return home early, while Papa took you to the park. However, an unfortunate incident occurred when Tara hurt her upper lip at the park, causing minor bleeding. Following Nani's advice, we resorted to a bit of sugar, and miraculously, the bleeding stopped.

After a much-needed nap, the real celebration began. You awoke to Vinay, Namita, Ria, Shriya, and Ravi singing "Happy Birthday." The excitement on Dhruv's face was priceless—he reveled in the attention. And Tara, your radiant smile as everyone sang showed pure joy—your eyes sparkled with delight. Seeing both of you respond in your own unique ways to being celebrated filled me with such tenderness.

You were dressed in your birthday finery—Tara in a pink and white dress and Dhruv looking dapper in a maroon "pathani" suit, both gifts from your Choti Nani. Once you were all dolled up, we cut the mango birthday cake from the Red Ribbon Bakery. Dhruv, your unstoppable enthusiasm for the cake was delightful—you kept asking for more with each delicious bite, and it quickly became your new favorite.

Organizing a birthday party for twins means everything comes in doubles — two little voices hearing "Happy Birthday," two sets of hands reaching for wrapping paper, two completely different reactions to the very same gift. Instead of trying to divide the moment, I found myself enjoying how it multiplied — more laughter, more surprise, more excitement filling the room at once. Watching each of you celebrate in your own way made the day feel fuller, brighter, and wonderfully alive.

The afternoon unfolded into easy laughter and scattered toys as you explored each new treasure with wide-eyed curiosity. By evening, Aditya, Kripa, and Aisha arrived with more surprises, stretching the celebration a little longer. Papa and I mostly stood back and watched — soaking in the noise, the chatter, the small bursts of joy — quietly aware that these ordinary moments would someday become the ones we miss the most.

You were surrounded by love in the form of thoughtful gifts. Hardik, Purba, and Ahona sent books and toys, while Dadi delighted you with teal scooters that immediately felt like prized possessions. Vinay, Namita, and Ria gave you the colorful table and chairs that soon became your daily station for coloring and little projects. Ravi and Shriya added to your growing library. Aditya, Kripa, and Aisha brought mega blocks and a doctor set — though the doctor set never made it to the playroom that day. We wrapped it back up and tucked it under your Christmas tree. We've learned not to open every birthday gift at once; some are saved for rainy days, some for strategic negotiations, and some for future celebrations. They also gifted you *Huggy, Kissy*, which quickly became part of our bedtime ritual. You adore Leslie Patricelli's books.

Your chote dadu and Choti dadi from Fresno gifted you

a chalkboard, and now we are regularly instructed to draw animals on demand. Tara, you especially love drawing your own face — two floating eyes, a smiling mouth, and a single straight line of hair across a triangle head. To us, it's perfect art — imaginative, confident, and entirely yours.

Happy 2nd birthday, my precious ones! These two years have been the most challenging and rewarding of my life. Watching you grow from tiny infants into these vibrant, unique individuals fills me with wonder every single day. I'm so grateful to be your mom.

Love,

Mom

December 27, 2023

Dear Tara and Dhruv,

Over the past few days, we've witnessed your special bond growing even stronger. Your affection for each other is heartwarming; if one of you gets a cookie, you immediately ask for another to give to your sibling. When playing, you prefer engaging with each other rather than snatching toys. It's endearing to see your camaraderie, especially when you team up against Papa and me in moments of mischief.

Yesterday morning, after Papa and I stepped out of the living room, Dhruv playfully closed the door behind us. I called out, "Tara te Dhruv kithe gaye?" ("Where did Tara and Dhruv go?") Dhruv opened the door, and both of you had the most beautiful and radiant smiles on your faces. We repeated this little game five times, and each time your excitement was just as infectious.

Life with twins is often wonderfully chaotic. Papa and I are almost always working — mentally and physically — negotiating turns, resolving tiny conflicts, preventing accidents, answering questions, and trying to keep the day moving forward. Sometimes, in the middle of all that motion, I just want to get somewhere quickly. But then you stop in front of every house to smell a flower, and I feel the familiar flicker of impatience because we've slowed down again. And yet, in those pauses, you remind me to slow down too. You teach me to notice small things — a petal, a breeze, a laugh — and to be present in a way adulthood often forgets.

The beauty of childhood lies in its innocence — relishing the little things and offering warmth so freely. Every day you gift us devotion, wonder, and perspective. Dancing together, making funny noises, your carefree movements — these moments make my worries dissolve and help me feel light and childlike again. Watching Papa smile like a child when he sees you dance fills my heart with contentment. I am grateful to you for bringing that back into my life, and I treasure these moments when you are thriving, healthy, growing, and strengthening your bond.

Another exciting development we've noticed is your growing passion for books. It's wonderful to see your curiosity and interest in stories, but it has also presented some new challenges. Lately, your enthusiasm for books has turned into quite an obsession. You've both started waking up in the middle of the night, crying for books. When it happened again last night, Papa and I were exhausted, so we let you sit on our laps and quietly flip through books without reading. You seemed content — until we suggested going back to bed, and you protested loudly, Dhruv: "I want book, I want book," with particular determination.

The challenge with twins is that when one wakes up demanding books, the other inevitably follows. There's no quietly soothing one child back to sleep while the other remains undisturbed. Instead, we're managing two determined toddlers who feed off each other's energy, escalating the situation until we're all wide awake at 2 a.m., surrounded by picture books in the dark.

To ease you back to sleep, we left the lights on and gave you three books each to read in your cribs. Dhruv even attempted to climb out of his crib to reach the book rack! But after a bit of crying, you both fell back asleep holding your treasures. Today, we all woke up quite late, as you can imagine!

Starting today, we are transitioning you to floor mattresses. This decision isn't directly related to the book obsession, but rather because you're both getting more mobile and we're worried about safety—especially after Dhruv's attempted crib escape last night! We're hoping the floor mattresses will give you more freedom to move around safely while still containing your nighttime adventures. Papa and I are crossing our fingers for smoother nights ahead, though we're prepared for an adjustment period.

Your passion for books, while sometimes challenging for our sleep schedules, is truly a gift. It's amazing to see how stories captivate your imagination and how eager you are to explore new worlds through pages. We're excited to nurture this enthusiasm for reading, even if it means a few more sleepless nights along the way.

Sending much affection and solidarity,

Your sleep-deprived mom

January 6, 2024

Dear Tara and Dhruv,

Your Nanu visited for two weeks during the end of December and into early January, coinciding with your holiday break from daycare, and brought such happiness to our home. It's a blessing to witness the special bond you share with him, as he engaged with you in various activities filled with focused attention and devotion. From building imaginative houses with Picasso tiles for your dog (Tara) and lion (Dhruv) to playing doctor and creating towering structures with Mega Blocks, your days were filled with laughter and wonderful moments. Papa and I also found moments of respite with your Nanu around. We even initiated your college savings plan this week – thinking about your future education already!

Christmas was a delightful celebration with our friends Ravi, Shriya, Reena, and Pranav joining us. Decorating the Christmas tree was a highlight, and you enjoyed coloring ornaments together. The festive feast included delicious samosas, dhoklas, bhel puri, and various baked goodies. While you two played around the house—occasionally "helping" by rearranging ornaments we'd just hung—the adults engaged in a lively game of Taboo, with Ravi and Shriya emerging victorious.

After the feast and games, we gathered to unwrap presents.

Dhruv opened *Boys Matter*, Tara received *Different Seasons*, and our friends happily opened the books they had been hoping for. Reena and Pranav gifted you *100 Chapatis*, and your daycare sent along a coloring book. You also finally opened the doctor set we had saved from your birthday, along with a puzzle toy. The excitement was instant — you both dove straight into your new books, flipping pages with eager curiosity. It was a day wrapped in warmth, laughter, and togetherness.

We all wore matching red sweatshirts, personalized with our names and featuring "#DhruvTara." I had ordered these custom-made from a website in India, and they were delivered to your Nanu, who brought them to the US during his visit. Wearing them together made us feel even more like a unit. We had a lovely photo shoot at a local park, capturing special moments in those sweatshirts. The pictures turned out wonderfully, and we're hoping to compile them into a photo book soon.

I'm writing this letter while Papa and your Nanu take you to the Children's Discovery Museum. I had to miss it due to a headache, but I'm feeling better now. It's one of those moments where having twins means missing out feels doubled - not only do I miss seeing your individual reactions to new exhibits, but I also miss witnessing how you interact with each other in that environment. But I need to get back to working on my dissertation before you return home.

Remember, we adore you immensely – always.

Hugs and kisses,

Mama

January 7, 2024

Dear Tara and Dhruv,

Happy New Year, my beloved babies. Every year people talk about fresh beginnings and new blessings, but for me the greatest gift of any year is simply the two of you.

We welcomed this New Year by leaving home for a few days — just our little family, along with your Nanu — and driving toward the coast. We stayed near Cayucos Beach, a quiet stretch of ocean not far from Paso Robles, where the air smelled of salt and everything seemed to move a little slower.

Before reaching there, we stopped in Monterey. The aquarium completely captured your attention. You pressed your faces close to the glass, watching fish glide past as if you were trying to understand their world. Three hours passed without any of us noticing. Later, while we wandered along Cannery Row, a little girl kept coming back to say "Hi" to you. Dhruv, you hid behind me at first, unsure, but soon the three of you were laughing and playing, strangers turned instant companions — the way children do so effortlessly.

That evening in Paso Robles, instead of settling indoors, we followed the sound of children's laughter to a playground still open under the night sky. The air was cold, but you refused to leave. Dhruv, you became determined to climb a smooth ladder you kept slipping from. After we took off your shoes, you tried again and again until you finally made it to the top, your face shining with triumph. We had stood in that very place months earlier when your Nani visited, and being there again felt like reopening a memory — this time with Nanu beside us, eager to see the places he had only heard about.

In the hotel room, the beds quickly stopped being beds and became trampolines. Traveling with twins means constant tiny negotiations — who sits where, who holds what, whose turn it is — a rhythm that now feels like part of daily life. That night we ate warm pizza and breadsticks from a nearby restaurant, and afterward walked through Sensorio, where fields of glowing lights stretched endlessly into the dark. You watched quietly, as if you knew it was something special.

The next morning you both looked especially sweet — Tara in the yellow woolen frock Dadi had knitted for you, and Dhruv in your striped shirt and orange-brown pants. On our way home we stopped in San Luis Obispo. We bought each of you tiny hand sanitizers that clipped onto your strollers — partly practical, partly a clever distraction when patience ran out.

At lunch you played with an animal-themed chess set while we ate. During the long drive back, Tara slept peacefully for most of the way, while Dhruv talked softly to yourself until sleep finally found you too. By the time we reached home, we were tired in the satisfying way that follows a full day — the kind that leaves memories behind.

I feel deeply blessed to have two little souls filling our home with movement and laughter. Raising you is a responsibility that humbles me, and every day Papa and I try to give you as much warmth and happiness as we can. You are, truly, our heaven-sent blessings.

Love you and bless you,

Your Mom, Jasleen

February 8, 2024

Dear Tara and Dhruv,

I want to share with you the new routine we've established over the past six weeks, ever since we moved your mattresses to the floor in early December. Every night, we have what I like to call our "family sleepovers" in your room. It's just the three of us - you two and me - and the experience has been truly wonderful. Papa sleeps in our bedroom since the twin mattress in your room isn't big enough for all four of us, but he joins us for bedtime stories and prayers before heading to his own bed.

Our sleeping arrangement is cozy and sweet. I sleep on a twin mattress in the center of your room, while both of you have your crib mattresses on either side. However, by morning, I often find you both sprawled across my mattress. Dhruv, you enjoy snuggling into my arms, and Tara, you use my stomach as your pillow. Some nights, I wake up as a human pretzel with little feet in my ribs and tiny hands in my hair, but I wouldn't trade these moments for anything.

The nights have been so much more restful now that I sleep with you! Whenever you have a nightmare or cry in the middle of the night, I can give you a soft pat while half-asleep, and you fall right back to sleep. Until a few weeks ago, you would wake up almost every night at 2 am crying, and we had to fully wake up, come to your room, and console you—leaving us all wide awake and disrupting everyone's sleep. Getting a full night's sleep is doing wonders for my body and mind, and you both love having me beside you too. Every night, we say our prayers, I sing for you, and we drift off to sleep. It's an incredible sensation—touching your warm hands, sensing how needed I am, and feeling deeply cherished.

Your growing language skills continue to amaze and inspire me. Your first sentences are heart-melting! Although we haven't captured some of these lovely phrases on video yet, hearing you say "What happen?", "Dhruv is crying" (using the full '-ing' form!), "Sleepy time", and "Happy Tu Tu" (for happy birthday) is precious beyond words! The way you're both starting to form complete thoughts and express them is remarkable.

These nighttime moments and your growing language skills are constant reminders of how quickly you're growing and how special this time is. Each day brings new words, new expressions, and new ways for you to show your unique personalities.

As I write this, I'm filled with gratitude for these quiet nights and bustling days with you. Your Papa and I treasure every moment, every new word, and every snuggle.

Lots of love and affection,

Your Mom, Jasleen

<h1 style="text-align:center">February 12, 2024</h1>

Dear Tara and Dhruv,

Over the past few days, I've witnessed a beautiful change in your play. You've begun taking turns with a toy, and it has been heartwarming to watch. This kind of cooperative play is new for you both, and seeing you learn to share fills me with quiet relief and happiness.

We've been playing with your Lovevery toy — the one with three wooden cylinders that drop through the holes when the plastic piece is pulled out. The three of us took turns while Papa was at work. Each of you would pick a block, hand one to me saying "Mama's," and give the third to each other. Then you'd encourage everyone: "Put it in!" Tara, you'd proudly say, "Tara's turn," and pull the piece out. Then it would be Dhruv's turn. The next day, while I was in the kitchen, I heard you doing the same with Papa, and it made me smile.

This moment meant more to me than just play.

For as long as I can remember, I have been your preferred parent. I know it is because I am the one you run to for comfort, and part of me loves that deeply — but it also carries a quiet guilt. I cannot hold you both at once. I cannot change your clothes or do your hair at the same time. Sometimes I wish you would prefer Papa, even just for a little while, so I could give each of you the undivided attention you deserve.

From the very beginning I have repeated one line to you: *"One mama, two babies."*

And another: *"We take turns in this house."*

You know these words now. You repeat them. But you are still so little, and I'm sorry you had to learn this so early. Some children get their parents entirely to themselves for years. You never did. You had to share me from your very first day, and I had to learn how to choose between two crying babies — something that took a kind of acceptance I am still learning.

Even today, when I hug one of you, my eyes search for the other. I find myself blowing kisses across the room so the other doesn't feel left out, repeating softly, "one mama, two babies." When you fight over a toy, you both cry — first for the toy, then because I take it away, and then because you both want comfort from the same person. Those moments are some of the hardest to navigate. So seeing you begin to take turns on your own felt like a small but meaningful milestone — a sign that sharing might finally be becoming real to you.

These are some of my favorite moments with you. Your growing vocabulary, the way you babble to yourselves, how you tuck your dolls in to "sleep" — all of it fills me with wonder.

Alongside these joys, we're also navigating challenges. Today I had a video appointment with Dr. Li, your pediatrician. Tara, you've been waking around 4 a.m., crying and wanting your legs massaged. I worried it might be the same pain you had months ago during Roseola. The doctor suggested it might be more about comfort than pain and advised trying a back rub instead. She was right — the back rub soothed you just as much.

Moments like these make me feel helpless in a different way. With twins, when one of you struggles, I immediately wonder about the other. Am I responding correctly to both of your different personalities? Am I giving each of you enough individual attention? You are learning so much at once — walking, talking, managing emotions, sleeping — and sometimes I wish I could remove every discomfort you feel. But I am learning that my job is not always to remove challenges, only to help you through them.

Know that Papa and I are always here — celebrating your growth and supporting you through the difficult parts too. Your resilience amazes us every day.

Love,

Your Mom, Jasleen

<h1 style="text-align:center">March 8, 2024</h1>

Dear Tara and Dhruv,

Happy Women's Day! With your daycare closed today, we spent the whole day together. Our morning began with a visit to Murphy Park, where you played with sand toys. The park was unusually quiet, likely due to it being the day when the grass was mowed. After an hour of sand play, we moved to Ben Rogers Park, where you both had a wonderful time playing together— giggling, chasing each other, enthusiastically tossing sand, and sliding down the slides.

As I watched you play, I found myself reflecting on how much has changed in just a year. Last spring, you were just learning to walk, and your Papa and I were constantly on high alert. We worried about you stumbling on the slide ladder, running towards cars, or suddenly dashing off in unexpected directions—all those typical toddler adventures that kept us on our toes.

I've always been someone who enjoys daydreaming and contemplating creative ideas. This introspection allows me to experience emotions deeply and engage in inner dialogues about the person I want to be – both as an individual and as your parent. Last year, I was so focused on your well-being that I felt a part of myself slipping away—the part that keeps me grounded and defines who I am. With twins, this feeling was especially intense because there was literally no time for myself. Every moment was accounted for: feeding one while the other cried, changing diapers in assembly-line fashion, managing two different nap schedules that rarely aligned.

Sometimes, when I went quiet to help calm the emotional chaos when you were cranky, I was called inattentive—even though my silence was protection, a way to create peace. When I was thinking creatively and took longer to complete a task, I was called slow—but this reflective pace was an important part of my personality that people didn't understand. This lack of empathy for a new mother, sometimes even from my own family, hurt me deeply.

Gradually, I'm rediscovering that part of myself. Now, I find time to think about these letters I'm writing to you, reflect on my work, envision our future, and imagine us as a content, harmonious family. This process of imagination fills me with energy and power.

Often, I catch myself singing and dancing to nursery rhymes, and it brings me such joy to see you following along, tapping your feet and moving your bodies. Our contentment is truly contagious—your delight brings me fulfillment, and my peace, in turn, makes you cheerful.

Last August, during a particularly challenging time, I reached out to your Aunt Jess, a dear friend and fellow mom living in America. She understands the unique challenges of being an immigrant mother, especially during the pandemic, and the specific expectations placed on Indian moms. I asked her how she handles misjudgments and lack of empathy despite her struggles. Her response has stayed with me: "I choose to ignore negativity, and that keeps me balanced. A peaceful mom means a thriving family." The wisdom in her words is now crystal clear to me.

One source of my well-being is the ability to immerse myself in contemplation. I've found this freedom for two reasons: first, as you've grown, I no longer need to be on constant high alert. Second, I've realized that this introspective time is an essential part of who I am and a wellspring of energy. So, I now consciously make time for myself.

The results have been remarkable, both mentally and physically. Every moment with you brings out the best in me. I feel calmer, more patient, renewed strength to navigate conflicts without becoming overwhelmed, and profound contentment. I savor our time together and find satisfaction in seeing the world through your eyes. Our shared laughter amplifies this sense of wellbeing. I'm grateful to your Papa too; we both prioritize "me time"—I take long baths while he watches you, he goes for solo walks while I handle bedtime—engaging in activities that rejuvenate us, fostering peace for ourselves and, by extension, for you.

These past two years since your birth have taught me so much, particularly about preserving one's identity amidst the whirlwind of parenthood. While change is inevitable and often necessary, it's crucial to safeguard the core aspects of yourself— the things that make you uniquely you. It's easy to let the world's expectations overshadow these facets. I experienced this loss of self during a challenging phase, and you might encounter similar feelings someday. If you ever read this letter in the future, remember: "Time has the power to heal many wounds. Persevere, and gradually, you'll find the energy to reconnect with your true self."

Your Nani is a remarkable example of strength and commitment to one's identity. Even now, she actively engages in various pursuits: writing, practicing yoga, attending meetings, contributing to the Gurdwara (Sikh temple) committee, and participating in community service for the elderly. Her life has been defined by dedication and sacrifice, particularly in raising us and advocating for our education despite a challenging childhood. While my own childhood wasn't perfect, I share these insights because your Nani played a crucial role in shaping who I am. I'm here in the U.S. largely because of her resilience – her refusal to accept limitations on what we could achieve. She helped me discover my identity, and even when I felt it slipping away, her unwavering dedication to her passions inspired me to reclaim my sense of self.

Your Dadi has inspired me in different ways. She has consistently made sacrifices for our family's well-being, a commitment she maintains to this day. What stands out about her is her ability to remain calm amidst life's challenges – a trait I also see in your Dad. Despite difficult situations, she always wears a smile, striving to maintain her equilibrium. She understands that a peaceful mother contributes to a thriving family.

As your mother, I aspire to find a balance between maintaining composure and patience and having the strength to stand up against injustices. I want to be a mother who protects her children from harm while also taking care of her own well-being. My hope is to inspire you both to pursue excellence in life, to be resilient in the face of challenges, and to always stay true to yourselves and your innate nature.

Love,

Your Mom, Jasleen

P.S. - You might have noticed that I've started including my name in recent letters. It's an essential part of my identity. While I treasure my roles as mom, wife, daughter, daughter-in-law, and friend, I am fundamentally Jasleen, and my name holds significant value in defining who I am.

<h1 style="text-align:center">March 9, 2024</h1>

Dear Tara and Dhruv,

Today we spent time at our friends' home, and you both immediately set off to explore every corner. New toys always seem to carry a special magic — you approached them with curiosity and delight, especially the little barn. You laughed as you opened the gate again and again, pulling out the pig, the horse, and the farmer like tiny treasures.

This playdate reminded me of another recent one, just two days ago, when your friend came to our house. It's beautiful to see how you're both developing social skills and enjoying the company of other children. These interactions are precious opportunities for you to learn about sharing, taking turns, and making new friends.

Beyond these fun playdates, I want to tell you how proud I am of you. Today, Dhruv, you accidentally bumped your head on the edge of a table and couldn't stop crying. Tara, you immediately went to your brother, gently stroking his hair to comfort him. In your softest voice, you repeated, "You are okay, you are okay." It melted my heart.

Moments like that remind me why Papa and I try so intentionally to model kindness in our home — not just by telling you to "be nice," but by showing you what it looks like. We believe children become what they see more than what they are told. If we speak gently, set boundaries respectfully, apologize when we are wrong, and comfort each other openly, you learn that this is how love works. And when I see you reflect that back to one another, I feel proud — of you, and quietly, of us too.

Lately, I've noticed how expressive you both are — your laughter, your tears, your strong opinions, your dramatic protests. There was a time when your big emotions overwhelmed me. When you cried hard or had long tantrums, I worried. I wondered if I was doing something wrong. Over time, I've begun to understand something different: you cry freely because you feel safe. You melt down because you trust that we will stay. You don't suppress yourselves because you don't have to grow up too quickly here. And that realization has brought me so much peace.

You certainly have your disagreements — sometimes intense ones — but even in the middle of those, there is connection. The hugs after. The checking on each other. The quick return to play. Papa and I treasure witnessing your bond grow.

Sometimes, when I think about your future, I find comfort in knowing you will always have each other. Tara, your willingness to compromise is beautiful, but I hope you always remember to stand tall when needed. And Dhruv, your determination is strong, but I hope you continue learning to soften it with empathy. Finding that balance between kindness and self-respect is something I am still learning myself.

There have been times in my life when I confused being kind with over-giving. My hope for you is different: that you grow into people who are generous and warm, but also clear about your boundaries. That you know how to say yes with joy and no with confidence.

I also want to say how proud I am of your Papa. He is an exceptional father and partner. His patience, his playfulness, and his steady presence make this home what it is. Managing twins means we are constantly tag-teaming — one soothing tears while the other redirects curiosity. We are not perfect, but we are intentional. And that matters.

I feel incredibly fortunate to be your mother. Watching you grow — not just taller, but kinder, braver, more expressive — is the greatest gift of my life.

With love and immense pride,

Your Mom, Jasleen

March 17, 2024

Dear Tara and Dhruv,

As I compile our family memories for this book, I realized there was a gap in my letters between December 20, 2022, and September 19, 2023, except for one letter written on April 27. So I want to revisit some treasured moments: your first birthday, your grandparents' visits, our trip to India, and the arrival of your little cousin, Ahona.

First Birthdays

We celebrated your birthdays with two wonderful parties in our apartment complex's community space.

A few days before your actual birthday, Tara wore a beautiful white and red dress, and Dhruv looked dapper in a brown waistcoat with matching pants, a white shirt, and a brown bowtie. These outfits were gifts from your Dadu and Dadi, who truly have a wonderful eye for children's fashion. Looking at the pictures now, you both were the sweetest babies in the world. I genuinely wish I could go back in time just to hold you both tightly again.

We invited many friends and family — Shriya and Ravi, Deep, Anu and her parents, Hitesh, Snehal and Kabir, Reena and

Pranav, and many others. The room filled with laughter, chatter, and warm wishes for you both. You received books to begin building your little library, clothes you would soon grow into, your first pair of stylish shoes, a swing set, and yes — many toys. But more than the objects themselves, it was the feeling of being surrounded by love that made the day special.

The celebration included pizza, cake, and special cupcakes made by your Dadi. She baked sugar-free banana cupcakes using almond flour, topped with yogurt frosting and strawberries — all your favorites. Your Dadi is known in Chandigarh for her cakes and cookies, and that day she brought a piece of that love into our celebration.

We played "passing the parcel," where an object is passed around in a circle while music plays, and when the music stops, the person holding it performs a dare. Some unforgettable highlights: Hitesh doing sit-ups while carrying Dhruv on his shoulders, Ravi balancing on one leg for twenty seconds — again with Dhruv on his shoulders — and me singing two songs for everyone. It was a day full of warmth, laughter, and small chaotic joys.

A week later, we hosted another party. Tara wore a green salwar-kameez, and Dhruv wore an off-white kurta pajama set. You looked like little movie stars. Our guests included Jessica, Nate, and their daughter; Sarah and her daughter; Simona and her son; Olga and her husband; and several friends of your grandparents.

There was a bit of drama when the pizza delivery arrived an hour late. Everyone was hungry and slightly frustrated — including you two, even though you weren't eating pizza! But that imperfection somehow made the day more memorable.

As I look back, what moves me most is not the decorations

or coordinated outfits, but the way our chosen family gathered around you. In a foreign country, far from our roots, these friends became our village — the people who would witness your milestones and become part of your story. That is the true gift of your first birthday.

Grandparents' Visits

Your Dadu and Dadi arrived in December 2022 just before your birthday, bringing abundant affection, gifts, and even some jewelry. A few days later, we marked my birthday by buying a new seven-seater SUV so that all of us could travel together comfortably — a practical but meaningful celebration.

We went on many family outings — two trips to Santa Cruz (once just the six of us and once with Nani later that month), visits to the Gurdwara, the Children's Museum, and Happy Hollow Zoo. Despite having just had a wisdom tooth removed and being on painkillers, I joined every outing. The discomfort felt small compared to the joy of being together.

Your Nani visited in December as well and saw you for the first time. She was overjoyed, pouring her love into every cuddle and play session.

Later that month, your father's uncle and aunt — whom you call Chote Dadu and Choti Dadi in our family tradition — visited too. We spent a lovely day at Stanford University, enjoyed crepes at a café, and visited the Great Mall.

The only set of grandparents who live close to us are another Chote Dadu and Choti Dadi in Fresno, along with their two teenage sons. You always have so much fun with them. I truly admire how much they enjoy spending time together as a family — how present they are with each other. We visited them in Fresno when you were about eight months old, and since then they have visited us several times. There is something comforting about having family within driving distance.

Trip to India

In late March 2023, when you were about a year and a half old, we traveled to India for nearly two months. We first stayed at Nanu and Nani's home. For me, it was a much-needed break after the challenges of postpartum life.

I cherished watching you with your grandparents and extended family — Mataji, cousin grandparents, aunts, uncles, and Lakkhi didi. You were surrounded by generations of love.

During our flight from Siliguri to Delhi, you charmed everyone. Passengers kept asking, "Are they twins? So cute!" You both delighted in walking up and down the aisle, exploring confidently even on the short Delhi-to-Chandigarh flight.

One moment I will never forget: Tara, you approached a young man wearing ripped jeans. You kept poking your finger through the rip in his knee and bursting into laughter. I gently brought you back to our seats multiple times, but you returned again and again, determined to investigate. The man smiled and said, "It's totally okay — this is funny. She's so cute." His kindness made the moment even sweeter.

In Chandigarh, you enjoyed mangoes straight from the tree, bowls of yogurt, and sunny baths on the verandah. We visited parks, and you played endlessly. You met many more relatives from both sides of the family. We even held a special prayer ceremony at the Gurdwara, where you captivated everyone present.

Ahona's Birth

In May 2023, your cousin Ahona was born — Hardik and Purba's beautiful daughter. Watching them become parents brought back vivid memories of my pregnancy with you.

At 34 weeks, I developed preeclampsia. Doctors recommended steroid injections to help your lungs develop in case of early delivery. I remember feeling the weight of that decision.

Even in the hospital, I immersed myself in medical papers and statistical evidence. I wanted to understand the risks and benefits fully before agreeing. That moment showed me the depth of a mother's devotion.

Education, in its truest form, gives us the ability to think critically and make informed decisions. It allows us to evaluate evidence, to question thoughtfully, and to feel confident that our choices are grounded in understanding rather than fear. Education opens the mind and helps us view the world from multiple perspectives. In that hospital room, I felt grateful for that ability — to analyze, to reason, and to decide from a place of knowledge.

These experiences shaped me profoundly. I placed your safety above relationships, above conventional advice, above my own comfort.

Motherhood transformed me in ways I never anticipated. Before you, I often tried to please others. But when it came to you, I found a strength I did not know I possessed. I stood firm.

I remember your Nani once saying, "You have changed."

At that time, I remained quiet. I didn't argue. But inside my heart, I knew the truth — I had changed. I had become a mother.

And in that role, I understood that nothing and no one could ever be as important to me as you, my precious babies — except, of course, your Papa. I often hear mothers say they love their children the most in the world. I understand what they mean, but I cannot say it that way. I love the three of you deeply. Each of you holds a place in my heart that no one else can occupy.

We even say it in our home, in the way that has quietly become ours:

"Who is my special girl?" — Tara.

"Who is my special boy?" — Dhruv.

"And who is my special man?" — Papa.

When I say it, I mean it. My heart did not shrink when I became a mother — it expanded. It made room for more love, not less.

This journey — from the anxious hospital days before your birth to welcoming your cousin Ahona — has shown me the depth of a mother's devotion. It transforms. It strengthens. It reshapes priorities.

As I watch you grow, I feel immense gratitude for the privilege of being your mother.

With love,

Your Mom, Jasleen

March 19, 2024

Dear Tara and Dhruv,

I wanted to share a couple of funny stories about Dhruv that I'm sure will make you both laugh when you're older.

One chilly day this winter, Dhruv decided he didn't want to wear any clothes at all! He cried and fussed until I helped him take everything off. Luckily, he agreed to wrap up in his favorite yellow and white blanket, a gift from your Choti Dadi from Fresno. He sat on my lap, all bundled up, for 30 minutes — even eating his dinner like that! We read books and watched some TV before he finally asked me to put his socks back on. I was so relieved when he started showing interest in getting dressed again.

Meanwhile, Tara, you watched this entire drama unfold with the patience of a saint, occasionally bringing Dhruv his toys as if to gently persuade him that being dressed might not be so terrible after all. You've always had this thoughtful instinct to help when your brother is being particularly determined.

Another time, last summer, we were heading to the beach when Dhruv threw a tantrum about not wanting to wear anything but his diaper. So, we decided to pick our battles and buckled him into his car seat wearing just his diaper for the entire 50-minute drive. To our amusement, he happily sang songs to himself the whole way there! Tara, you kept looking over at him with an expression that seemed to say, "Really, Dhruv? This is what we're doing today?" We have some hilarious pictures of that car ride. Tara, if you ever need material to tease your brother when you're older, just ask us.

These moments, while sometimes exhausting in the moment, are part of what makes parenting such an adventure. They remind me how strong-willed and spirited you both are. Dhruv, your determination can be astonishing. Tara, your quiet patience — and sometimes your subtle amusement — balances him in ways I don't think you even realize yet.

But alongside the laughter, there is also the constant unpredictability of these years. Not just in clothing choices, but in moods. In tantrums. In not always knowing what might set one of you off — hunger, tiredness, a toy taken away, a word misunderstood. Some days feel like gentle breezes; others feel like navigating sudden emotional storms. We are always learning — reading your cues, adjusting, responding, trying to stay calm when big feelings take over small bodies.

And yet, even in that uncertainty, there is beauty. Because your emotions are real. Your reactions are honest. You are still learning how to regulate a world that feels very big to you.

I cherish how these little incidents — the diaper drives, the blanket dinners, the dramatic protests — slowly transform into stories we can laugh about. They are proof of the wonder, the unpredictability, the moods, the messiness, and the laughter that fill our days as a family.

Love,

Mom, Jasleen

P.S. Dhruv, I hope you don't mind us keeping these stories for posterity. They're told with nothing but devotion and affection.

97

March 22, 2024

Dear Tara and Dhruv,

Today turned out to be one of those unexpectedly full days — the kind that begins with something routine and ends with muddy shoes and tired, happy faces.

Our morning started with Mama and Papa's annual health checkup, which included a blood draw. We woke up early, got ready, and left at 7:30 a.m. Dhruv, you carried the toy syringe from your doctor set, and Tara, you brought your toy stethoscope. I quietly hoped that letting you "participate" in our checkup might make the experience feel less intimidating, especially remembering how hard past blood draws have been for you.

When it was time, I went first. Papa brought you both in to watch, and you stood there wide-eyed, repeating, "Mama-injection, Mama-injection." Once I was done, Tara, you confidently said, "Dhruv's turn," showing how deeply the idea of taking turns is settling into you — even in situations that might feel scary. You both observed carefully while Papa had his turn. And when we were ready to leave, Tara, you didn't want to go — you were still waiting for your own turn, eager to be part of it all.

You both handled the morning beautifully. Dhruv, you looked

so sweet in your blue and white poncho that Dadi sent. Tara, you were glowing in your pink and white woolen dress from Kawal Masi. With your tiny doctor instruments in hand, you brought smiles to an otherwise quiet hospital lab. There was a small baby there, and Tara, you kept calling her "Ahona." You've been so excited about your cousin that every baby seems to remind you of her.

Afterward, we stopped at our favorite diner for breakfast. We ordered omelets, bacon, and pancakes — but somehow, the butter seemed far more fascinating than the pancakes themselves.

Later in the day, we decided — almost on a whim — to visit Deer Hollow Farm. It was cold and rainy, but that didn't stop us. You wore your frog raincoats, and when the rain started coming down harder, we let you walk instead of staying in the stroller.

You had a blast.

You jumped from puddle to puddle, giggling loudly. People stopped to watch the two little "frogs" splashing in the rain. Your shoes and socks were completely soaked, but you didn't care at all. The puddles were irresistible.

Managing two excited toddlers in the rain while filming little videos and making sure no one slipped was a challenge — but watching your joy made it worthwhile. Papa and I just kept looking at each other and smiling.

The day reminded me of our visit to ArdenWood Farm in Fremont last weekend. You fed chickens and sheep, laughing when the sheep licked your hands. We made small sheep crafts using real wool, ribbons, and pipe cleaners. We created two tiny sheep and took so many pictures. Before leaving, you fed goats too.

Days like these stay with me. Not because they are grand

or perfectly planned, but because of the way you experience them — fully, joyfully, without hesitation. Your excitement over puddles, animals, butter, and toy syringes reminds me how simple happiness can be.

I look forward to many more days like this — muddy, special, and full of life.

Love,

Mom (Jasleen)

March 25, 2024

My Dearest Tara and Dhruv,

As I sat watching an episode of NCIS, I couldn't help but be captivated by Special Agent Leroy Jethro Gibbs. At around 60 years old, this NCIS special agent chooses not to use a smartphone. In a conversation with Phineas, another character in his early teens, Gibbs expresses his perspective on letter writing. He shares that he believes it to be challenging and a lost art, surpassing the convenience of messaging any day. I wholeheartedly agree with him. It took me back to the time when I was in a long-distance relationship with your dad—for about eight months after we met in May 2019, he was in Boston while I was in Austin. We'd meet every two weeks, alternating who would travel, until March 2020 when the pandemic hit and I moved from Austin to Boston to be with him. During those months apart, we exchanged handwritten letters. Those letters remain treasured keepsakes, carefully preserved in a special box that I hope to share with you someday.

Much like the letters I write to you now. These letters serve as a tapestry of precious moments for you, weaving together a narrative that brings deep satisfaction to my heart. Each time I capture a moment in words, I find solace in the knowledge that I'll never forget it – that I can revisit it anytime. Writing down these memories automatically brings a smile to my face as I envision the delight these recollections will bring to your faces when you walk down memory lane. Perhaps you'll consider a particular episode as a thrilling escapade—a shared adventure between siblings.

The act of writing these letters brings me fulfillment. In capturing the beauty of my little ones, I momentarily forget any sadness in my life and find myself smiling. These letters serve as a reminder of the wonderful people in my life, especially you—my little ones who never cease to amaze me with your adorable antics, giggles, and the wonder of watching two tiny creatures navigate the world. Gratitude fills my heart for the life I have.

Finding time to write with twins is no small feat—I often scribble notes on my phone during your naps, then transfer them to proper letters when you're asleep. Sometimes I write while you're having your morning milk, stealing those quiet moments to capture yesterday's memories before they fade.

If I can offer you both a piece of advice—on those tough days when the world seems to let you down, when the struggles feel overwhelming, write it down. Even when writing about your worries doesn't ease them, write about something that doesn't burden your thoughts. Write about a tree outside your window, a cloud in the sky, a classmate, or even the Prime Minister of New Zealand.

In a world where mental health faces unprecedented challenges, may you find solace and peace in the simple act of looking outside your window and writing about it!

I adore you, treasure you, and am grateful for you, my precious babies!

With all my love,

Your mom, Jasleen

P.S. - The episode is Season 18, Episode 14 (Unseen Improve-
ments), approximately 25 minutes into the episode. Maybe
one day we'll watch it together, and you'll understand why it
inspired me to write this letter.

March 26, 2024

Dearest Tara and Dhruv,

Our home has been full of small, delightful moments lately, and I want to capture a few before they slip into memory.

Tara, you've developed a fascination with the mirror — especially when you're wearing something new. Dhruv, you sometimes join in, but it's safe to say your sister takes the lead in this department. A couple of nights ago, I styled Tara's hair into two ponytails with little braids. At first, you were wiggly and impatient, but when I gently said, "Tara, I'm making pretty hair," you suddenly sat still, letting me finish. The moment I was done, you ran to the mirror, looked at yourself carefully, and declared, "Pretty hair!" The next morning, you insisted on showing Dadi and Nani on our video call, turning your head from side to side so they wouldn't miss a single braid. Your pride was so pure.

Yesterday, we bought new shoes for both of you — bright green and black pairs that light up with every step. This became necessary after the purple ones surrendered completely to the puddles at Deer Hollow Farm. You both ran around the house, watching your reflections and stomping just to see the lights flash. Dhruv, you refused to take yours off at bedtime. Every attempt to remove them was met with loud protests, and eventually we gave up. So you slept in glowing shoes. I endured a few accidental kicks to the face during the night, but even that felt like part of the story we'll laugh about later.

Watching you admire yourselves in the mirror made me think of something I saw recently. A mother shared that whenever her children dress up and look nice, she calls them "fancy." But when they do something brave, kind, or compassionate — something that reflects who they are inside — she compliments their inner beauty. She said it's important to celebrate effort and feeling special, but even more important to remind children that true beauty is about who they are as human beings.

That stayed with me.

So now, when you dress up, I tell you that you look fancy — because you do. Your clothes, your neat hair, your light-up shoes — they are fun and joyful and worth celebrating. But I also tell you that you are beautiful all the time. Not just when your hair is braided perfectly or your shoes are shining. You are beautiful when you share. When you comfort each other. When you say sorry. When you try again after falling. When you laugh freely. When you show kindness without being asked.

You are fancy in your outfits.

But you are beautiful in your character.

With twins, these expressions of individuality feel even more meaningful. While Tara admired her hair, Dhruv carefully lined up his toy cars in perfect order. When we bought the shoes, Tara wanted to show everyone immediately, while Dhruv was busy testing every light-up feature. You approach the world differently, and I love witnessing that.

This morning, during our video call, we proudly showed the new shoes to Dadi, Dadu, Nani, and Nanu. Moments like these shrink the distance between us and your grandparents, letting them share in your everyday excitement.

These incidents may seem small, but they form the fabric of our life together. Tara, your growing self-awareness and pride are beautiful to see. Dhruv, your stubborn determination and enthusiasm are equally wonderful. As your parents, we find joy in guiding you — not just in how you look, but in who you are becoming.

May you always enjoy dressing up.

May you always stomp in glowing shoes. (Though I do hope you eventually take them off. If not, I suppose we'll have a built-in nightlight for a while — and knowing you, that's entirely possible.)

But most importantly, may you grow into humans whose inner beauty shines far brighter than anything you wear.

Lots of love,

Mom, Jasleen

April 14, 2024

Dear Tara and Dhruv,

There's so much I want to share with you, and I wish I had all the time in the world to do so. My heart skips a beat when you look at me as if I'm the only person you want in this whole wide world. I'll never forget Dhruv's mischievous smile when he's about to do something naughty. Yesterday at the Gurdwara, he kept walking toward the microphone, turning his head around and smiling at us, daring us to stop him.

But I also want to tell you something honest.

Dealing with your tantrums can be emotionally draining. Sometimes, I find myself hugging your Papa, tears streaming down my face. I express my frustration when you insist on wearing a specific jacket or socks that aren't appropriate for the weather or occasion. There are moments when the constant demands and noise overwhelm me, and I wish I could retreat to a quiet room for just five minutes without being needed. The relentless nature of parenting can sometimes feel suffocating.

With twins, this exhaustion feels magnified in ways I never anticipated. Managing two simultaneous meltdowns, two different needs at the exact same moment stretches me in ways I never imagined. There is rarely a pause. If Dhruv needs something, Tara inevitably needs something else at that same moment. The math often feels impossible — two children, two hands, one overwhelmed mother. Some days I have whispered to Papa, "I can't do this anymore," only to have you both look at me with such pure love that I remember why I always will.

What hurts deeply are the comparisons. When people say, "You're so lucky to have twins! You're done in one pregnancy!" I sometimes want to laugh. They don't see what it means to gain forty pounds, to develop preeclampsia, to carry the near certainty of premature babies and the medical anxiety that comes with it. They don't see the postpartum fog that lingers for years. They don't see the exhaustion that doesn't quite leave your bones.

As first-generation immigrants in the U.S., we are doing this without the support systems many others rely on. Your Papa returned to work one month after you were born. I continued my PhD with no maternity leave. There was no year-long parental leave, no subsidized childcare, no affordable domestic help like in India. We were navigating twins in a system not built to support families — and certainly not families without nearby relatives. When family members compare us to parents of single children and say other couples seem more "relaxed," it cuts deep. It makes exhaustion feel like a personal failure rather than a natural response to an overwhelming situation.

And yes — sometimes I feel envy.

When parents of single children talk about being tired, a small part of me thinks, "You have no idea." I have felt guilty for thinking that. I have wondered what kind of person feels both blessed and resentful at the same time.

But here is what I have learned.

The grass is always greener on the other side. Some parents envy us for not having to go through pregnancy twice. But I will never know what it feels like to be pregnant again while raising a toddler. I will never know what it feels like to bring home a newborn and simultaneously guide an older child through that transition. Every path carries its own weight. Every story has its own invisible struggles.

Motherhood has humbled me. Since becoming your mama, I have gone out of my way to help other mothers. Sometimes that means listening while they vent. Sometimes it means sharing my story so they feel less alone. Sometimes it's bringing food or essentials. Sometimes it's just sitting beside them. Once you understand how heavy this role can feel, you cannot unsee it in other women.

A friend once told me something that changed the way I see myself: we are human, and it is possible to hold two feelings at the same time. There can be two truths in one story.

So here are mine:

I am deeply blessed.

And I am deeply exhausted.

I sometimes feel envy.

And I also feel compassion.

Both are true. And I am learning that acceptance — not comparison — is where peace lives.

The emotional exhaustion of being a mother, especially a mother of twins, is real and rarely acknowledged. Now that you've grown so much, I can only hug one of you at a time — and my heart aches every time I have to choose which of you to embrace first. When you both declare "My mommy!" and compete for me, I sometimes wish I could split myself in two. That is one of the hardest parts — loving you equally and physically not being able to show it simultaneously.

And yet.

Despite all of this, despite the exhaustion and the moments when I feel like I'm drowning, I often find myself transported back to your newborn days. I remember how you would stare into my eyes with pure innocence and trust as I sang to you. Your favorites were "Nindiya Re" by Kaavish, "Sooha Saaha Amma Ka" from the movie *Highway*, and the kirtans by Shivpreet Singh. Those moments were quiet and sacred.

If you were born one generation earlier, you would have grown up surrounded by cousins in Chandigarh and Ludhiana. Instead, your Papa and I chose to build new lives in new countries to create opportunities for you. That choice has meant distance from siblings, parents, and extended family. We are raising you largely without the traditional "village."

But something unexpected happened.

In this foreign land, our friends became our family. The people we see more often than relatives — the ones who stood beside us through sleepless nights, illnesses, academic stress, and emotional overwhelm — they are family in every way that matters. Especially with other mothers, there is an unspoken understanding. A look that says, "I get it." They have seen us at our most exhausted and stayed. That kind of presence is a gift.

And through all of it — the venting, the comparisons, the immigration stress, the exhaustion — there is something that remains constant.

My love for you.

I miss the days when you both fit easily in my arms and I could hold you together, feeling your tiny hearts beat against my chest. But I also treasure watching you grow into your own little people. I want you to know that my affection for you is infinite and equal. There is no competition in my heart. You both hold irreplaceable places there.

Your Papa and I are doing our best. We are imperfect. We are tired. We are learning. But we are deeply devoted to you.

As parents, we are willing to sacrifice so much to raise you, and our greatest wish is that you grow into content, grounded, compassionate human beings.

Jasleen

April 17, 2024

Dear Tara and Dhruv,

As I sit here, just a week away from defending my PhD dissertation, I find myself reflecting on the incredible journey that brought me to this point. My pursuit of a doctorate in Public Policy led me to the United States, where I've been exploring the impact of women project leaders on project performance at the Asian Development Bank. This research was inspired by my experiences working with J-PAL (the Abdul Latif Jameel Poverty Action Lab), where I first became fascinated by women's roles in decision-making and implementation.

During my time with J-PAL, I had the privilege of visiting remote villages across Madhya Pradesh, Odisha, and Lucknow states of India. The women I met there left an indelible mark on my heart. They welcomed me into their homes, sharing their stories over tea and lunch. Their hospitality was humbling— some even used their emergency funds to buy milk for our tea or brewed it with water they had collected from miles away under the scorching sun. These encounters taught me about humility, finding hope in adversity, and the inherent beauty and kindness in the world.

The past six years have been transformative. I've grown from a single, somewhat naive girl into a woman with two beautiful children—you—and a husband who supports my dreams. I've built a family, both professionally and personally, with significant overlap between the two. My dissertation mentors have been incredibly supportive throughout this journey. Kate, my chair, has been an exceptional advisor, guiding me through all transitions. She affectionately calls you "Tooter" and "Beans," names from children's books she's working on. Her devotion and support, shown through guidance and gifts, have been invaluable.

Completing this PhD while raising twins has been one of the most challenging things I've ever attempted. There were countless nights when I worked on my dissertation after you both fell asleep, only to be interrupted by midnight wake-ups and early morning demands. I've written research papers while you napped, attended virtual conferences with you playing quietly nearby, and somehow managed to maintain my academic focus despite the beautiful chaos you bring to every day. The traditional image of a PhD student—solitary, uninterrupted study time—became a luxury I had to reimagine entirely.

Another pillar of support has been the WhatsApp group "Indian Moms in the US." This community of Indian mothers navigating parenthood in a new country has been my safe haven. Whether I needed to vent or seek advice about baby-related issues or academic struggles, this group has always been there with judgment-free, sound guidance. Their unwavering support has been a blessing.

I also joined a book club when you were about a year old, discovered through another new mom on a "Buy Nothing" Facebook group. These groups, which connect people offering or seeking free items, have become lifelines for mothers like me. What started as a simple book recommendation became something much more meaningful—a monthly escape from the world of toddler conversations and endless "why" questions. After days filled with discussing favorite colors, snack preferences, and playground adventures, gathering with a group of thoughtful, articulate women to dive into complex literature felt like returning to a part of myself I had nearly forgotten. These monthly discussions, where we dissect characters' motivations and debate themes over wine and cheese, provide the intellectual stimulation I crave. More than that, they've helped me build genuine friendships with other mothers navigating similar challenges of raising children far from extended family. The book selections consistently surprise and challenge me, and sharing insights with these intelligent, accepting women has become a sacred ritual that nourishes both my mind and spirit.

However, this journey has also been marked by losses. Shortly after I arrived in the US, we lost my paternal grandfather. The pandemic brought more heartbreak, with the loss of many friends and family members. The most profound loss was that of my cousin. His untimely death due to Covid-19 left a void in our hearts. Memories of our childhood, the songs he played in his BMW, and moments like my engagement ceremony, where he made me feel like a princess, now carry a tinge of sadness without his presence. On your father's side, we also mourned the loss of several near and dear ones. I was pregnant with you during this time, and being in the US, I felt a mix of sadness and gratitude. The strict safety measures and the diligence of those around us in following protocols provided some comfort.

This was the first time in my life that I had experienced death in the family, but in the years since, I've undergone significant personal growth. Life has evolved like the changing seasons, shedding some aspects while nurturing others. Despite the inevitable losses, this process of growth and change brings a certain beauty to life.

But the lessons I've learned have not only come from academia or from grief. Some of the hardest lessons came during my most vulnerable season—becoming a new mother to twins. I was stretched thinner than I knew possible. Physically exhausted. Emotionally raw. Hormones raging. Identity shifting. I was at the most fragile point I had ever been.

And vulnerability teaches you things.

I learned who stays.

I learned who quietly disappears.

I learned who stands beside you.

And I learned who smiles in front of you but speaks differently once you leave the room.

There are, I've come to believe, three kinds of people in this world.

There are those rare ones who truly understand, who are empathetic in their bones, who allow you to emotionally regulate safely in their presence. They hold your secrets with care. They protect your vulnerabilities.

Then there are those who listen, nod, and move on. You are not maliciously judged—but you are also not truly held. You are simply not an afterthought.

And then there are those who listen with compassion in the moment—but later share your postpartum depression, your medical information, your struggles, without consent or regard. Your vulnerability becomes conversation.

I learned that lesson the hard way.

And something in me shifted after that.

Even if someone belongs to the first category now, I find myself unable to open up fully. When people ask, "How are you?" I almost always reply, "Life is great. I count my blessings every day." And the truth is—I do. I have the best husband and children I could ever ask for. I am deeply grateful.

But there is also a part of me that changed postpartum. Something that softened before and then hardened after. Sometimes it feels like something died. Other times, it feels like I simply developed a survival tool—a way to move through the world without exposing every tender part of myself.

These are lessons we don't learn in classrooms.

I wish for you to encounter many "type one" people in your lives—those who hold space gently and guard your stories. But I also know your lives will include a mix. And me explaining these categories to you will not protect you from the experience of discovering them yourselves. You will learn your own lessons, in your own time, through your own heartbreaks and awakenings.

My only hope is this: that you trust me enough to be your "type one."

I hope I can be the safe place where you can bring both your light and your shadows. The victories and the embarrassments. The mistakes and the secrets. It takes intention as a parent to hold back constant advice, to resist fixing everything, to allow you to emotionally regulate in your own way. But your journey is yours.

My role is not to control it—only to walk beside you.

I pray you learn your lessons without losing too much of your softness. I pray the world is kind to you. And I pray that even when it isn't, you carry enough strength, wisdom, and joy to build beautiful lives.

As I approach this milestone, I'm filled with pride, gratitude, and deep appreciation for how much I've grown. You, my dear children, are the most precious result of this journey. Through all the challenges and triumphs, you have been my constant source of inspiration.

May you always find the strength to pursue your dreams, the courage to face life's challenges, and the wisdom to appreciate both the happiness and sorrows that shape your lives.

With all my affection,

Your Mom, Jasleen

April 24, 2024

Dear Tara and Dhruv,

Yesterday marked a monumental milestone in my life—I successfully defended my PhD, culminating six years of relentless hard work. The moment was intense, filled with nerves that left me oscillating between hot and cold. Despite the whirlwind of emotions, I gave it my all, and I'm relieved and proud to say that I passed.

In the aftermath, many suggested celebrating with a nice meal, ample sleep, a vacation, or even a massage. Instead, I chose a different path. I spent two hours in bed, allowing myself to release years of pent-up emotions through tears. The overwhelming gratitude I felt toward the wonderful individuals in my life mingled with the sheer mental and physical fatigue accumulated over these challenging years.

This journey has been marked by numerous hurdles—adapting to life in a new country, navigating different cultures, forging new relationships, embracing motherhood, battling postpartum depression, and confronting patriarchal pressures—all while diligently pursuing my PhD. Doing it all while raising twins made every aspect exponentially more difficult. Yesterday became a cathartic outlet for all these experiences.

Interestingly, I found myself applying the strategies I've learned for managing your "big toddler feelings" to my own emotions. I practiced self-soothing, releasing feelings that had been building up long before you came into my life. Amidst the relief of unburdening myself, I also grappled with not feeling entirely proud of my achievement, haunted by the feeling that I could have done better.

Your Papa, ever supportive, entered the room with words of encouragement that touched my heart. He sees me through a lens of admiration—a strong, vibrant woman balancing significant responsibilities while nurturing our beautiful family. Though his words resonate deeply, years of societal conditioning make it challenging to fully embrace my achievements.

I also called my dear friend Anu. We spoke about the show *This Is Us*—a poignant portrayal of devotion, loss, and resilience across generations. But what made that call meaningful was not just the show. During some of the toughest points in my life, I have called Anu while sitting in my car, crying uncontrollably. And she would say, calmly and firmly, "I am here. Let's cry." She would sit with me through it. Then she would guide me: "Take a deep breath. Drive carefully back home. Go to your room. You don't have to talk to anyone. Just sleep." And because I was emotionally and physically exhausted, I followed her instructions exactly. The next day would feel a little lighter. And then lighter still.

Friends who can hold you steady when you are falling apart— who stay calm when you cannot—are rare and precious. They do not fix you. They anchor you. And that kind of friendship is something I hope you both experience in your lives.

But you know what truly made this day beautiful and meaningful? You, my dear children.

When I picked you up from daycare, your sweet voices filled the air with excitement. Your Papa playfully asked you to say, "Doctor Jasleen." Dhruv, you charmingly replied, "Doctor Gasleen Mama" (yes, Gasleen!), then thoughtfully offered me a piece of the celebratory muffin your Papa had baked. Tara, ever considerate, brought out your toy doctor set, opened it up, and sweetly exclaimed, "Congrats, Mama."

My heart melted at the sight—my entire life gathered into that moment. It was a moment where Doctor Jasleen looked at her beautiful babies and her incredible husband, all smiling, giggling, and simply enjoying being together.

It's the mornings when Tara wakes up and cups my face in her tiny hands and says, "Mama, Mama, Mama."

It's the nights when Dhruv insists, "Mama here, Mama here," before falling asleep.

It's the times when you both boss me around—telling me where to sit, where to stand, even when I'm allowed to use the bathroom!

It's the way you look at me as if I am everything to you.

This—our family, our connection, our shared chaos and comfort—is a treasure beyond compare. You are my greatest gift.

As I close this chapter of my academic journey and open new ones, I'm filled with gratitude, fulfillment, and quiet excitement for what lies ahead. Thank you, my sweet children, for being the brightest lights in my life and the steady heartbeat behind everything I do.

With all my love, always and forever,

Your Mama, Dr. Jasleen

Epilogue

Writing these letters has become my quiet sanctuary—a cherished practice where heart meets paper and memories take permanent form. As I close this collection, I find myself regularly returning to these pages, each re-reading bringing fresh emotions and forgotten details back to life.

These written conversations with Tara and Dhruv have become an unexpected gift to myself as well. In documenting their growth, I've witnessed my own transformation alongside them. From the overwhelming uncertainty of those early twin days to the profound satisfaction of completing my PhD while raising two toddlers, these letters have captured my evolution. Not just their milestones, but my journey as a mother, a woman, and an individual striving to maintain her identity amidst the beautiful chaos of parenthood.

Through these pages, I've learned to embrace the authentic struggles of twin motherhood—the exhaustion that society doesn't acknowledge, the impossible mathematics of two children to two hands, the loneliness of feeling misunderstood even by those closest to us. But I've also captured the extraordinary moments that make it all worthwhile: synchronized giggles, the way they comfort each other, and those fleeting instances when everything aligns perfectly despite the chaos.

I share these letters now, hoping they might resonate with others navigating their own parenting journeys, especially those raising twins who often feel isolated in their experiences. To the mothers who whisper "I can't do this anymore" in moments of desperation, to the parents who feel guilty for not feeling "blessed" every single moment, to the families building new lives far from their roots—you are not alone.

This practice of letter writing has taught me that preserving our stories matters. In a world of quick texts and fleeting social media posts, there's profound power in putting pen to paper, in creating something permanent that captures not just what happened, but how it felt. These letters have become my way of saying to Tara and Dhruv: "You were seen. You were celebrated. Every moment of your childhood mattered enough to be remembered."

But this isn't the final chapter—my journal continues to fill with new letters as our family story unfolds. As the twins grow into their own unique selves, there will be new challenges to navigate and fresh milestones to celebrate. I hope our extended family of cousins across continents will grow closer despite the distances. There will be more stories to tell, more moments to preserve.

Perhaps someday, these future letters will find their way to bookshelves as well. For now, I remain grateful for this practice that anchors me through the beautiful chaos of motherhood. It preserves today's small moments that will become tomorrow's most treasured memories and reminds me that even in the midst of twin mayhem, there is profound beauty in the ordinary magic of raising children.

To every parent reading this: your story matters. Your struggles are valid. Your love is enough. And sometimes, the simple act of writing it all down can transform the overwhelming into the meaningful, the chaotic into the cherished.

With love and solidarity,

Jasleen

Acknowledgments

I am deeply grateful to the remarkable women who have shaped both this book and my journey as a writer and mother.

My mother, Tara and Dhruv's Nani, Inderjeet Kaur, is a writer who instilled in me a love for words. Her belief in storytelling and her unwavering encouragement gave me the courage to put pen to paper and preserve our family's story.

My mother-in-law, my second mother, Virinder Kaur, has the rare gift of preserving memories. She carefully saved keepsakes and childhood treasures, and watching Danvir see our children play with his old toys is a joy beyond words. She inspired me to document and safeguard these fleeting years.

I am equally grateful to Anushree — my first roommate in the United States when we began our journey at UT, and my very first friend as we navigated this new life as international students. Over the years, she has been a steady presence through some of the hardest seasons of my life. Her calm, grounded strength and her ability to simply "be there" always reminds me of the power of true friendship.

To my PhD advisors — Kate, Raissa, Erin, Diane, Soledad, and Mirko — thank you for guiding me with both rigor and kindness. You saw the person behind the scholar and supported my growth not just academically, but personally.

Soledad Prillaman deserves special acknowledgment. She gave me my first professional home and helped me see the world

— and women's empowerment — through a deeper lens. Her influence extends far beyond my research; it shapes how I lead, how I think, and how I mother.

I am thankful to my developmental editor, Mozelle J., whose thoughtful guidance helped shape these letters into a cohesive book. I am also grateful to Susan Barkan — my book club friend — for reviewing and proofreading the manuscript and offering invaluable feedback in its final stages.

My sincere thanks to Darsana Thulasi, whose line art for the cover brought this book to life with elegance and depth. Her artistry captured the spirit of these pages in a way words alone could not.

To my circle of mom friends — women who truly "get it" — thank you for your honesty, humor, and solidarity. I am grateful for the nannies, babysitters, teachers at daycare who have loved and cared for my kiddos. A single thank you is not enough to express how grateful I am for holding the fort.

And finally, nothing in my life can be acknowledged without honoring the love of my life — my husband, Danvir Singh Sethi. Thank you for walking beside me in parenthood, for contributing your own letters to this book, and for being a steady, loving presence in our home. You make me a better mother and a braver woman.

www.ingramcontent.com/pod-product-compliance
Lightning Source LLC
Chambersburg PA
CBHW071753150726

47998CB00005B/1923